What Presbyterians Believe

An Interpretation of the Westminster Standards

by

JOSEPH M. GETTYS

Professor of Bible

PRESBYTERIAN COLLEGE

CLINTON, SOUTH CAROLINA

BOOKS BY JOSEPH M. GETTYS

Leader's Guide for What Presbyterians Believe
How to Teach the Bible
Teaching Others How to Teach the Bible
How to Enjoy Studying the Bible
Teaching Others How to Study the Bible
How to Study Luke
How to Teach Luke
How to Study John
How to Teach John
How to Study Acts
How to Teach Acts
How to Study I Corinthians
How to Teach I Corinthians
How to Study Ephesians
How to Teach Ephesians
How to Study the Revelation
How to Teach the Revelation
Surveying the Pentateuch
Teaching the Pentateuch
Meet Your Church
Leader's Guide for Meet Your Church

First Printing, February, 1953

Fifteenth Printing, January, 1963

Dedicated to my daughter Jean
With a prayer that she may learn in her experience
the meaning of the Presbyterian Faith

Preface

PRESBYTERIAN STUDENTS in college often get into "bull sessions" with their friends and feel embarrassed because they do not know what they believe. They know that theirs is a doctrinal church, but they do not know how to define or to give reasons for their faith.

Likewise chaplains in the various branches of the armed services are appalled at the spiritual ignorance of the men they seek to serve. Other groups may know what they believe, but few Presbyterians do.

In many local congregations ministers and educational leaders are seriously hampered in their work because some of their members have learned a mixture of Presbyterian and non-Presbyterian theology and insist upon teaching the mixture to the children and youth of the church.

In every age and every area of life, Presbyterians are revealing a lack of moral and spiritual stamina such as that which comes from a faith clearly understood and firmly held. They are not different from other church members in this respect, but they might be helped by a better understanding of what is contained in their official doctrinal standards. While as members of the church they are not required to accept these standards for admission, as parents and officers they do profess to subscribe to them.

In the fall of 1952, the author began a four-year experiment at the First Presbyterian Church in Dallas, Texas. In this experiment he sought to discover what would happen to people in a local church who took their educational program seriously. The first volumes of his "How to Study the Bible" series were then available. It became clear that materials for adult electives must be clear in content. They must be pedagogically effective. They must be accompanied by suitable teacher's or leader's guides. The search for a text in "What Presbyterians Believe" as a basic course ended in disappointment. A number of texts dealing with general beliefs of Christians were examined, but none sufficiently set forth the doctrines contained in the Presbyterian Standards. Other books which interpreted Calvinistic theology, including one on the Presbyterian Standards, did not seem to serve as good study texts for lay people. It became necessary therefore to produce a text for which a leader's guide might be prepared in order to provide a suitable text for a basic course in our curriculum for older young people and adults. This series of studies, arranged in thirteen units, is designed for this number of class periods. If necessary, combinations may be made to fit into a ten-hour study.

It will become evident from the outline, which is provided in detail because no index is included, that an attempt has been made to include all of the basic doctrines of the Presbyterian Standards. The selection and interpretation would doubtless be different with another author. However, it is hoped that the selection is comprehensive and the interpretation both clear and reasonably accurate. Obviously all Presbyterians cannot be lumped together as though none of them thought for themselves. A freedom in thought and a loyalty to the scriptural faith which makes Presbyterianism a glorious heritage among Protestant bodies is fully recognized. The primary goal of these studies is to present the point of view of the Westminster Standards, and to permit those who differ to differ in the peace and harmony of Christian love.

Two chapters, one dealing with our task in the home and another with our task in society, are included because of the peculiar needs of American Presbyterianism. If these chapters do not properly interpret the spirit and the letter of the Presbyterian Standards, they may at least point a direction in which Presbyterians are moving. Some, of course, are far ahead of others. The presentation is purposely conservative in the hope that those who lag behind in these areas of thought and conduct may be moved to join others who are striving to work out their faith in these special areas of human living.

Any advanced theological student who reads these pages will discover quickly that this is an introductory type of study for lay people. The fine points of speculative or dogmatic theology that appeal to advanced students are avoided in the effort to present the main points of Presbyterian faith clearly. However, many of the controversial questions that concern lay people are dealt with in relation to the Presbyterian Standards. It is hoped that the presentation is fair and that the spirit of love is apparent. Additional reading will be suggested from time to time in the leader's guide.

Who is expected to use this study book? Older high school and college students, young adults and adults who would understand their faith more clearly, and individual church members who desire a book on the faith of Presbyterians will probably find this book helpful. Some ministers may wish to guide study courses with the faithful members who attend Sunday evening services or study classes. In this case, it is important that two things be done. One is to get a study book in the hands of every pupil or every couple so that preparation may be made in advance of the study period. Worksheets should be filled out *before* the class hour. In addition, opportunity should be provided for participation in the study period together, either through group discussion or through the use of questions before or after a lecture. It is highly important that pupils be encouraged to ask questions about matters that are not clear or not acceptable to them. Good theology should not become fruitless through poor pedagogy. Therefore care should be taken to bring the best in teaching to this cooperative learning experience.

Contents

CHAPTER I

Our Heritage as Presbyterians

INTRODUCTION

THE ROOTS OF PRESBYTERIANISM are in the Bible. The name comes from the Greek word presbuteros, translated elder. It points back in the Old Testament to the elders selected by the tribes as their leaders (I Kings 8:1-3; Judges 8:14, 16; Deuteronomy 27:1; Ezra 10:8; etc.) In the New Testament church it is used to describe the overseers of a local congregation (Acts 14:23; 20:17; Titus 1:5). Both in the name and in the spirit of Presbyterianism, the Bible plays a central and significant role.

Our purpose in this chapter will be to present briefly the organization of the Presbyterian church and to indicate a few of the highlights in its history.

A. THE ORGANIZATION OF THE PRESBYTERIAN CHURCH

A Presbyterian church is a church governed by elders elected by the congregation and organically related to other churches. It differs from the Roman Catholic church which is under the authority of its pope and its hierarchy of church officials. In the Roman church, authority comes from the top downward to the people. Presbyterian church organization differs also from that of the Methodist and Episcopal churches, where authority centers in the Conference and Council made up of clergymen from these respective faiths. It also comes from the top downward to the people. Presbyterian church organization differs from the congregational form of church government(such as is represented by the Baptist churches) in that no Presbyterian congregation is a law unto itself. Each Presbyterian church is organically related to the Presbytery in which it is located. Authority in congregational churches resides in the congregation alone. Authority in Presbyterianism resides in the duly elected representatives of the congregation in the appointed church courts, which will now be discussed.

1. THE SESSION

The lowest church court is the *Session*. The Session consists of the pastor or pastors (teaching elders) and the ruling elders elected by the congregation. All pastors and associate pastors must be elected by the congregation and not by the Session. Assistant pastors, stated supply pastors and temporary pastors may be elected by the Session. Local congregations determine for themselves the number of members who shall be elected to the Session. In the United Presbyterian Church, U.S.A.

women as well as men are eligible for this office. In the Presbyterian Church, U.S., only men are eligible. The requirements for this office are set forth in the Book of Church Order.

2. THE PRESBYTERY

The next church court is the *Presbytery*. The Presbytery is composed of all ministers and one ruling elder from each church within a certain district, except that a church whose membership exceeds 1,000 is represented by an additional ruling elder for each additional 1,000 or major fraction thereof. This tends to keep the number of ministers and ruling elders equal in the Presbytery. The Presbytery has general supervision of all the Presbyterian churches within its given district. The Presbytery's Commission on the Minister and His Work grants the local congregation permission to call a minister but the Presbytery itself has to approve the call and install the minister. The Presbytery also dissolves pastoral relations and exercises authority over all of the ministers and churches within its bounds. It alone can organize or dissolve a church. A study is being made at the Assembly level concerning the rights of local congregations concerning church property. Ordinarily the property of dissolved churches in a Presbytery reverts to that body.

3. THE SYNOD

The third church court is the *Synod*. It consists of all the ministers and one ruling elder from each church in three or more Presbyteries. Steps have been taken to make the representation to Synod conform to that in the Presbytery in larger churches. The 1956 Minutes of the General Assembly of the Presbyterian Church, U.S. showed a total of 16 Synods and 85 Presbyteries. The Synod usually follows state boundaries but does not split Presbyteries where they comprise parts of two states. In many phases of the work of the church, such as stewardship, church extension, and higher education, the Synod formulates policies and exercises authority over the Presbyteries within its bounds.

4. THE GENERAL ASSEMBLY

The highest church court is the *General Assembly*, which is composed of one minister and one elder for every 5,000 communicants in each Presbytery. The Presbytery elects the delegates or commissioners to the Assembly and sends communications and requests called *overtures* to the Assembly. The Presbyteries vote on any major change proposed at the Assembly and a second Assembly must ratify an action approved by three-fourths of the Presbyteries (two-thirds in the U.P.-U.S.A. church). The General Assembly is the final court of appeal in the Presbyterian Church.

5. DEACONS AND TRUSTEES

Two questions frequently asked about Presbyterian Church organization should be answered. One concerns the function of deacons and trustees in the Presbyterian church. Deacons are officers in local congregations, elected by the people, who perform the functions similar to those suggested in Acts 6. They encourage stewardship of possessions, dispense the benevolent giving, provide for the current expenses of the church, maintain the church property, and serve the needy in the church and community. They may serve on special committees elected or appointed by church courts, but are themselves under the jurisdiction of the local Session. Trustees are elected for specific purposes designated by a local congregation or a larger church court. Their primary function is to hold in trust the properties committed to their care by the body under which they serve.

In the United Presbyterian church, U.S.A., the Finance committee of the Session often exercises functions normally left to the deacons in the Presbyterian Church, U.S. The trustees are more active concerning church property and generally have more authority. Persons who are members of that branch of the Presbyterian church should consult with their pastor or officers about the functions of these respective offices.

6. PRESBYTERIANISM AS A NEW TESTAMENT FORM OF CHURCH ORGANIZATION

Another question frequently asked is whether Presbyterians follow the form of church government in the New Testament, where the word bishop as well as the word elder is used to describe church officers. The truth of the matter is that the word translated bishop was first used as a synonym for the word translated elder (See, for instance, Acts 20:28 and compare the words here with those in Acts 20:17 and Titus 1:5). The function of such officers was that of overseeing the life and work of the church in a given community. Because of the limited number of ministers available during the first three centuries, an apostle or minister was called upon to serve a group of churches. Timothy and John served the churches of the Ephesian area. As time went on, this pattern was continued and the senior minister of an area was the overseer of the churches in that area. In this way the title of bishop was transferred from local elders to the senior minister of the churches in a given area. This practice led to the Episcopal form of church government, with its bishops and lower clergy. It may therefore be maintained that while Presbyterians may not dogmatically claim that no other form of church government is suggested in the New Testament, theirs reflects most accurately the form of church government established in the early church.

B. SOME HIGHLIGHTS IN THE HISTORY OF THE CHURCH

The following pages are highly condensed, and should be read slowly and thoughtfully. A few of the more important dates are suggested below and a chart showing relationships of American Presbyterian churches is given at the end of this chapter. Both should be consulted frequently to provide a framework for understanding the brief summary that is given.

1. Key Dates and Events

35 or
37   First Council at Jerusalem.

50   Second Council at Jerusalem.

590   Western church under dominance of bishop of Rome; Eastern church becoming a separate body.

1073   Pope Hildebrand claims to be head of whole church, with right to crown and uncrown kings.

1302   Pope Boniface asserts that spiritual power belongs to the church, and that temporal power should be wielded for the church.

1517   Martin Luther posts ninety-five theses on church door at Wittenburg, and leads the Protestant Reformation.

1533   John Calvin is converted to Protestantism, and soon begins his historic work at Geneva.

1559   John Knox returns to Scotland to organize the Presbyterian church of Scotland.

1643   The Westminster Assembly begins its more than five years of meetings, and produces the Presbyterian Standards.

1705   The Presbytery of Philadelphia is organized as the first Presbytery in the American colonies.

1717   The Synod of Philadelphia, Presbyterian Church of America, is organized.
1741   Division into New Side and Old Side over evangelistic fervor and methods, and plan of education for the ministry.

1758   Reunion of the Synods of Philadelphia and New York into one Presbyterian church.

1789 Formation of national church with the title, "General Assembly of the Presbyterian Church in the United States of America."

1801 Union with Congregational churches during the rapid expansion to the west.

1810 Withdrawal and organization of the Cumberland Presbyterian church over issue of educated ministry. Cumberland church in pioneer territory where advanced education was thought unnecessary.

1837 Old School rejects former union with Congregational churches, and New School holds on to it. Church divides on this issue.

1857 New School, mostly in west, divides again over issue of slavery. The United Synod of the Presbyterian Church withdraws to form a southern branch of Presbyterianism.

1861 In reply to Gardiner Springs resolution opposing slavery and requiring support of the Federal government, the southern delegates withdraw and form the Presbyterian Church in the Confederate States of America.

1865 The two southern branches, the United Synod of the Presbyterian Church and the Presbyterian Church in the Confederate States of America, unite to form the Presbyterian Church in the United States.

1870 The two northern branches, the Old School and the New School, unite again as the Presbyterian Church in the United States of America.

In addition to these dates affecting the two larger branches of Presbyterianism in America, the student should consult the chart given at the end of this chapter. It will show the formation of other branches of the Presbyterian family, including the Reformed Presbyterian Church, the Reformed Presbyterian Church in North America, the Associate Reformed Presbyterian Church, and the United Presbyterian Church. The United Presbyterian Church and the Presbyterian Church in the U.S.A. united in 1958 to form the United Presbyterian Church in the U.S.A.

[13]

With this skeletal outline in mind, let us turn to discuss some of the highlights of the history of the church as it is related to our Presbyterian heritage.

2. THE EARLY CHURCH

The first general Councils of the Church were held in Jerusalem. They are described in Acts 11 and Acts 15. The Roman Church now claims that Peter was made the head of the Church by Christ Himself (interpreting the neuter petra in Matthew 16:18 to refer not to the conviction expressed but to Peter himself). It is claimed that Peter took this position as the first bishop of Rome in A.D. 42. This is not supported by Peter's denial, by the fact that James rather than Peter was the person of authority in the Jerusalem church (Acts 15:1-29) about A.D. 48-50, by Paul's boldness in withstanding him to his face in Antioch (Galatians 2:11) or by the absence of a greeting to Peter in Paul's letter to the Romans about A.D. 57. This theory actually was used as propaganda to support the claims of the bishop of Rome for supremacy over the bishop of Constantinople several centuries later and has remained ever since.

The exact form of local church government established by Paul and the other disciples did not persist during the days when the books of the New Testament were being collected and recognized as inspired writings during the second, third and fourth centuries. This was the period of the great church fathers and the historic church Councils. Cyprian, the bishop of Carthage who suffered martyrdom in 258 A.D., went so far as to say; "The bishop is in the church, and the church is in the bishop, and if anyone is not with the bishop, he is not in the church." As some bishops came to have more power, they established five centers in Rome, Constantinople, Alexandria, Antioch and Jerusalem. With the rivalry already mentioned between bishops, there was a division into the Eastern church, which became the Greek Orthodox church, and the Western church, which became the Roman Catholic church under the bishop of Rome. By 590 A.D., this bishop claimed and secured virtual control of the Western church.

This control was made complete under Hildebrand, Pope Gregory VII, in 1073. Hildebrand claimed to be head of the whole church. He claimed the right to crown and uncrown kings. Pope Boniface in 1302 asserted not only that the spiritual power belonged to the church, but that the temporal power should be wielded for the church. Along with the struggle for temporal power there was a deterioration in Christian doctrine and practice. The worship of Christ through angels and the Virgin Mary, the practice of praying people out of a purgatory (which

[14]

was believed in as a place of purging after death), the emphasis upon five more sacraments than Christ instituted, and the general corruption of the clergy marked the church life of the middle ages.

3. The Protestant Reformation

After several reforming groups under such men as Wycliffe and Huss had done their work, the Reformation broke out in Germany. Inspired by his re-discovery of the truth of God as he read the scriptures, Martin Luther, a Roman Catholic priest, nailed ninety-five theses to the door of the Castle Church in Wittenburg, Germany on October 31, 1517. This challenge to debate was occasioned in part by the offers of an agent of the Roman church named Tetzel who was selling indulgences (promises of immunity from future punishment in return for contributions toward the construction of St. Peter's church in Rome) in Germany. For nearly thirty stormy years, aided by Melancthon, Luther led the Reformation in Germany. Luther stood squarely on the authority of God revealed in the Bible as opposed to the pretensions of authority by the pope.

John Calvin, the father of modern Presbyterianism, was also trained in the priesthood, law, Latin, logic and philosophy. (The work of Zwingli, who as a contemporary of Calvin did much for the Reformed Churches, is not discussed for lack of space.) Calvin was converted to Protestantism in 1533 and published the first edition of his *Institutes of the Christian Religion* at the age of 26 in 1536. Under the pressing invitation of William Farel, John Calvin settled in Geneva in 1536 and began his reforms. After being driven out in 1538, he returned in 1540 and established Presbyterianism in thought and practice in Geneva. Geneva thus became the center for Reformed theology and church government for the continent and the British Isles. The key to Calvin's thought is his effort to interpret the scriptures as the authentic revelation of a sovereign God. He went back through Augustine to Paul and the Bible for both his theology and his form of Government. *Modern Presbyterianism is therefore a rebirth of the New Testament church.* It emphasizes theology, worship, education, thrift, ethical practice and representative government. Presbyterianism spread rapidly from Geneva to France and to Holland and other parts of the continent.

4. Persecution and the Flight to America

During the period when Protestants were being so severely persecuted in England and Scotland by Bloody Mary, John Knox, who had formerly been a galley slave in a French ship as a result of persecution, fled to Geneva and learned Calvinism first hand. He returned to Scot-

[15]

land in 1559 to organize the Presbyterian Church of Scotland. Amid his labors and tears he prayed, "O God, give me Scotland or I die!" His prayer was partially answered when he organized the first General Assembly of the Presbyterian Church in Scotland. The Roman Catholic monarchs of England and Scotland persecuted Presbyterians and other Protestants in Scotland, Ireland and England until many of those who survived came to America. A similar persecution, more ruthless and devastating, was carried on by the Romanists in France. The Massacre of St. Bartholomew's Day in 1572, in which nearly 100,000 Protestants were killed in various parts of France (simply because they were Protestants) sent many of the surviving French Huguenots (who were Presbyterians) to our shores. In a real sense it may be said that Presbyterianism came to America to escape the ruthless persecutions of Roman Catholic rulers, encouraged by the Roman church to which they gave their allegiance.

5. THE WESTMINSTER ASSEMBLY

One historic landmark in Presbyterianism in England was the Westminster Assembly which met at the call of a Puritan Parliament on July 1, 1643, and continued in active session for five years, six months, and twenty-two days. The six Presbyterian commissioners from Scotland, while denied an official vote, exercised a strong influence on the work of this Assembly. It started out to revise the doctrines, the worship and the living of the Church of England. It ended with the historic documents we know as the Directory for the Public Worship of God, the Confession of Faith, the Larger and Shorter Catechisms, and the Psalter. The Confession of Faith and the Catechisms, with minor modifications, serve as the doctrinal guide for Presbyterians in America to the present day. Ministers and officers are required to subscribe to these before ordination to their respective offices. Members are required only to recognize their need of the Savior, to commit their lives to Him, and to support the life and work of the church. While they are taught the Scriptures and the Christian faith in many ways, they are not required to subscribe to a specific set of beliefs in order to become members of the Presbyterian church.

6. THE ESTABLISHMENT OF PRESBYTERIANISM IN AMERICA

Presbyterians in America were first organized in 1705 or 1706 by Francis Makemie into the Presbytery of Philadelphia. There were seven ministers and "certain elders" present at this meeting. Presbyterianism grew among the colonists until in 1741 there was a division into the Old Side and the New Side in what had become the Synod of Philadelphia. The younger ministers, led by Gilbert Tennent, became flaming evangelists. This did not suit some of the older heads among Presbyterians, so the New Side evangelistic Presbyterians organized themselves into the Synod of New York. After the growth of the church in all of the colonies, these two sides were reunited in 1758. Having contributed to the spirit of freedom which lay behind the American Revolution, the Presbyterians met and organized "The Presbyterian Church in the United States of America" in May, 1789, just three weeks after George Washington was inaugurated as the first President of the United States. At the time there were approximately 177 ministers, 431 churches, and 20,000 members in the Presbyterian Church in America. This does not include some of the smaller bodies to be mentioned later.

In 1801 there was a cooperative union between the Presbyterian and Congregational churches which permitted ministers of the two churches to exchange pulpits and pastorates. While this resulted in the rapid growth of Presbyterianism, it also resulted in an action of the Assembly of 1837 (in which the Old School had the majority as the New School had in 1836) which declared the union null and void, cut off the four western synods of the Presbyterian church and caused a split into the Old School and the New School Presbyterian churches.

7. THE NORTHERN AND SOUTHERN BRANCHES OF PRESBYTERIANISM

Although the Methodists and Baptists had split over the question of slavery in 1845, the Presbyterians remained intact until the New School Presbyterian Assembly passed some drastic resolutions condemning slavery and led to the organization of "The United Synod of the Presbyterian Church." As if three groups were not enough there came another split in the Old School. In 1861 the Old School Assembly met in Philadelphia and passed, by a vote of 156 to 66, the Gardiner-Springs resolution, which reads as follows:

"That this General Assembly, in the spirit of Christian patriotism which the Scriptures enjoin and which has always characterized this church, do hereby acknowledge and declare our obligation to promote and perpetuate, so far as in us lies, the integrity of these United States, and to strengthen, uphold and encourage the Federal government in the exercise of all its functions under our noble Constitution; and to this Constitution, in all its provisions, requirements, and principles, we profess our unabated loyalty."

The War between the States was on at the time and very few of the delegates from the eight states which had seceded were present. Had the Presbyterians in these states subscribed to such an ill-timed resolution at the time, they would have been forced to leave their homes and forsake their communities. History has proved the value of the union of states. It is perhaps unfortunate that it has not seen the healing of the wound which led to the organization of the Presbyterian Church in the United States, (which was first called the Presbyterian Church in the Confederate States of America), at Augusta, Georgia, on December 4, 1861. The United Synod of the Presbyterian church united with this church in 1865, and the Old School and New School in the North reunited in 1870. This left only two of the four groups separated. The work of the Executive Committees and Boards at home and abroad, the growth of the larger branches of Presbyterianism in numbers, stewardship and in influence is an occasion for thanksgiving. According to recent statistics, the Presbyterian Church in the United States numbered approximately 900,000 and the United Presbyterian Church in the United States of America numbered approximately 3,750,000.

8. OTHER PRESBYTERIAN BODIES IN THE UNITED STATES

There are also several other distinctly Presbyterian bodies in the United States. Among these are the Associate Reformed Presbyterians in the South with a membership of approximately 30,000, the Cumberland Presbyterian Church, which has approximately 80,000 members, the Colored Cumberland Presbyterian Church with about 30,000 members, the Reformed Presbyterian Church with approximately 6,000 members, the Reformed Presbyterian Church in North America with about 1,500 members, the Orthodox Presbyterian Church (from which the Bible Presbyterian Church split off) with about 15,000 members.

Since the union of the Presbyterian Church in the U.S.A. and the United Presbyterian Church in 1958, there are only two large Presbyterian bodies in the United States, their combined total numbering approximately 4,350,000.

Therefore, when asked who Presbyterians are, we may reply that they are a branch of the Church universal whose roots are in the Old Testament, whose form or organization is set forth in the New Testament
lurch, whose freedom to think and to live according to the scriptures was reclaimed under John Calvin and John Knox and many others who died for their Protestant faith. There are several Presbyterian bodies in America. The three largest have a friendly relationship with each other.

Fuller details, of course, should be given about the history of Presbyterians. A part of this curriculum in the Dallas plan is a course in church history based on Dr. Walter Lingle's book, "Presbyterians,

Their History and Beliefs." The purpose of this brief summary has been to provide perspective for the study of Presbyterian beliefs, which are based on the Bible and have come to us mainly through Augustine, Calvin, and the Westminster divines.

We have a glorious heritage written in the blood of saints and martyrs. Let no one be ashamed to say he is a Presbyterian. But let every Presbyterian be ashamed to blemish a heritage won at such great cost to those who have made Presbyterianism something glorious in the history of the Christian church.

England   Scotland   Ireland

Groups from these coun

1752
Reformed Presbyterian
Church

1754
Associate Presbyte
Church

1782
Union of groups
from both
Associate Reformed
Presbyterian Church

Reformed
Presbyterian
Church

Associate Presbyte
of Pennsylvania

1801
Associate Synod
North America

1833

Old Light

*Reformed
Presbyterian
Church*

New Light

*Reformed
Presbyterian
Church in North
America
(General Synod)*

1822
Associate Reformed
Synod of the South

*Associate Reformed
Presbyterian Church*

1858
Union
*United Presbyter
Church of North
America*

Indicates Current Church Groups

Data not shown:

1869   Split from Cumberland Presbyterian Church to form Colored
           Cumberland Presbyterian Church

1906   Union of part of Cumberland Presbyterian Church with Pres-
           byterian Church in the U.S.A.

1936   Withdrawal of Orthodox Presbyterian Church from Presby-
           terian Church in the U.S.A.

1938   Withdrawal of Bible Presbyterian Group from
           Orthodox Presbyterian Church

France   Holland

led in American Colonies

1706
Presbytery of Philadelphia organized

1717
Synod of Philadelphia, Presbyterian Church of America

1741
Split over new Evangelism

Old Side opposed   New Side for
Synod of Philadelphia   Synod of New York

1758
Reunion
Synod of New York and Philadelphia

1789
General Assembly of the Presbyterian Church in the
United States of America

Congregational
Churches   1801
Union during
Expansion to the West   Education of ministry
1810
1837   *The Cumberland
Former Union with   Presbyterian Church
Congregational Churches

Rejected by Old School   Accepted by New School

1861   1857
Slavery, support of   Slavery, support
Union   of Union

Presbyterian Church
in the Confederate
School   States of America   New School   The United Synod of
rthern)   (Southern)   (Northern)   the Presbyterian
                                                        Church (Southern)
8

1870   1865
Union   Union
*United Presbyterian Church in   *Presbyterian Church in
the United States of   the United States
America   (Southern)

[21]

WORKSHEET

1. A Presbyterian church is a church governed by_____
   and related organically to other_____churches.

2. The four church courts of the Presbyterian church are:

   a. The_____, composed of the pastor and the elders of the
      congregation.

   b. The_____, composed of the ministers and one ruling
      elder from each church in a given district or area.

   c. The_____, consisting of the ministers and one ruling
      elder from each church within a larger area, usually following
      state boundaries.

   d. The_____ _____, consisting of one minister and
      one elder for every 4,000 communicant and members in each
      Presbytery.

3. Deacons and trustees are also elected by the congregation to look
   after church property, to encourage_____, and to serve
   the_____.

4. The first general Councils of the Church were held in_____.

5. By the third Christian century there were five strong bishoprics in
   the church. These were at_____, _____,
   _____, _____, and_____.

6. Popes_____and_____secured for the
   Roman church almost complete control over the life of Europe during the Middle Ages.

7. Martin Luther began his reforming movement in October,_____.

8. _____ _____, who settled in Geneva in 1536, is the
   person who, more than any other, restored worship and conduct to
   conform to the teachings of the scriptures and revived the Presbyterian church government.

9. _____ _____ learned about Presbyterianism from
   Calvin at Geneva and organized Presbyterianism in Scotland.

10. The French Huguenots and the Scotch and English Presbyterians settled in America primarily to escape_____from the _____ _____.

11. The Confession of Faith, and the Larger and Shorter Catechisms, which contain the system of doctrine taught in the scriptures, were produced by the_____ _____of 1643-1649.

12. Presbyterians in America were first organized by_____ _____.

13. The Old Side and New Side Presbyterians differed over the question of_____in the churches but were reunited in 1758.

14. The Old School and the New School Presbyterians divided, and each of these passed resolutions regarding_____which resulted in the United Presbyterian Synod and the Presbyterian Church in the Confederate States of America. These combined to form the Presbyterian Church in the United States, popularly called the Southern Presbyterian Church.

CHAPTER II

Our Rule of Faith and Life

INTRODUCTION

In answer to the second question of the Shorter Catechism inquiring how we may glorify and enjoy God, we have these significant words:

"The word of God, which is contained in the Scriptures of the Old and New Testaments, is the only rule to direct us how we may glorify and enjoy him."

Thus we have stated one of the fundamental principles of Protestantism. We bow to no pope, no council, no man or group of men, but rather before the sovereign God who speaks through the scriptures. As stated in the Confession of Faith, Chapter I, Article X:

"The Supreme Judge, by which all controversies of religion are to be determined, and all decrees of councils, opinions of ancient writers, doctrines of men, and private spirits, are to be examined, and in whose sentence we are to rest, can be no other but the Holy Spirit speaking in the Scripture."*

Presbyterians have kept this fundamental principle of the authority of God speaking through the scriptures as a significant cornerstone of their faith even when many philosophers and theologians have surrendered it in an appeal to human reason. Let us therefore strive to understand more clearly what Presbyterians believe about the Bible.

A. THE BIBLE CONTAINS A REVELATION FROM GOD

There are some Christians who dislike an interpretation of the Catechism statement which recognizes that the word of God *is contained* in the Scriptures. They prefer to say that the Bible *is* the word of God. Both points of view should be defined carefully by all who use them, for words often become very misleading.

Let us begin with the point of view of the Bible, which is the point of view of *revelation*. By revelation we mean that God discloses to man those things necessary for man's salvation. The Bible does not speak of "the development of the idea of God." It rather says, "in the beginning, God—." God creates a universe which reveals His glory. God acts in human experience and in history. God calls His leaders to service. God reveals Himself in Jesus Christ. God speaks through the Holy Spirit. We shall define this point of view more fully in the next

---

*All references by chapter and article are to the edition of the Confession of Faith which includes amendments of 1944.

[24]

two lessons. Suffice it to say here that the Bible is not a series of stories containing man's best thought about God. It is rather an inspired record of God's continuous disclosure of Himself to man. This is part of what we mean by *revelation*.

B. THE BIBLE IS AN INSPIRED RECORD OF GOD'S REVELATION OF HIMSELF TO MAN

We shall consider the nature of man in another lesson. It might be asked, how did Abraham or Moses, or Elijah, or Isaiah, or Micah, or John or Paul know that God spoke to them? How did the Hebrews know that the voice on the Mount was the voice of God? Sinful men do not always recognize God or understand what He is trying to say to them. No matter how great the disclosure of God, there had to be a way for men to know what God meant to say through His disclosures.

1. INSPIRATION

This brings us to the doctrine of *inspiration*. The word *inspired* means breathed into. A New Testament passage, II Peter 1:21, states that no prophecy of scripture ever came into existence by the impulse or will of man, but that holy men of God were moved to write by the Holy Spirit. This is to say that holy men, who were given peculiar insight by the Holy Spirit, understood something of God's revelation of Himself and interpreted that revelation to their fellow men.

These inspired men discovered God revealing himself "at sundry times and in divers manners." In spite of the primitive and limited understanding of God in early Old Testament times or later Old Testament times, God was speaking ·to His people. The hearing was often poor or badly interpreted. So Abraham had more than one wife and David took Uriah's wife away from him. But Abraham's self-made plans backfired and in his experience David learned from God that he had done wrong. When taken in larger segments, the Old Testament story, with all of its limited understanding of God, reveals more and more clearly the character and the will of God. In the prophets there is a clearer word and in Jesus Christ we find the final word. Hence the New Testament writers, standing in the light of Jesus Christ, reflect a clearer understanding of the redemptive love and will of God. This point of view, which is suggested but not developed in Chapter I, Article I of our Confession, is sometimes called "progressive revelation." The term is not too good, for there was one unchanging God revealing Himself all along. But there was a progressive *understanding* of God's revelation under the guidance and inspiration of the Holy Spirit. In the first place, therefore, inspiration provides for a growing understanding of God's self-disclosure.

[25]

Inspiration also extends to the *means of communication*. God communicated in ways that the Hebrews would understand and in ways that Christians could understand. This communication was in the form of acts which had redemptive meaning. But inspired writers had to communicate to their fellows. This they did through language, which is an inadequate but very helpful means of transmitting ideas. The Old Testament was written in Hebrew because that was the language known to the Hebrew people. It was a spoken more than a written language, though it was a written language long before the time of Ezra in 457 B.C. The vowel forms were not included in the language of the Old Testament, but were supplied by Hebrew scholars in the sixth and seventh Christian centuries. For this reason it is sometimes hard to know exactly what the original writer (or the compiler) intended to say. The Isaiah and Habakkuk scrolls recently discovered near the Dead Sea, are a part of the earliest Hebrew manuscripts of the Bible now in existence.

Because the Greek language had spread to all parts of the Roman empire in the time of Christ, the New Testament was written in the Greek language. Our earliest manuscripts, except for fragments such as the Chester Beatty papyri, were copied in the fourth and fifth centuries. By the science of textual criticism, some scholars have been able to arrive at what is the most likely original. It should be said that with all of the variations in existing manuscripts, no fundamental doctrine of the Christian faith is affected. God has spoken and God still speaks in the Bible with a voice of authority.

Inspiration is also believed to extend to the *selection* of the books of the Old and New Testaments. The list given in our Confession is the list that we know in our Bibles. Apocryphal books are excluded because they are not believed to have been inspired in the same sense that the other writings are. While most Presbyterians would use favorite books and passages because they are more helpful than others, they would include for study only those generally accepted, namely, the thirty-nine books of the Old Testament and the twenty-seven books of the New Testament.

2. PRESERVATION

The activity of the Spirit of God is also believed to have been made possible the *preservation* of the books of the Bible. This means the preservation of their essential truth and the preservation of the books—in spite of the fact that we do not have the original copies.

3. TRANSLATION

Closely related to inspiration and preservation of the Bible is the question of *translation*. Since Presbyterians believe that every man has

[26]

the right and the duty to study the scriptures, they also believe in translating the scriptures into the native tongue of believers. They have participated in the task of translating the Bible into approximately eleven hundred tongues and dialects. But most of them do not believe that a single translation, such as the King James or the Revised Standard Version, is inspired as over against the rest. While it is true that much is gained in translations from the original languages, something also is lost in rendering different shades of meaning. While therefore it is unsafe to make generalizations, it is perhaps fair to say that to a limited number of Presbyterians, the Confession means to say that the Bible *is* the word of God, word for word and letter for letter in the original languages (and virtually in their own favorite translation); but that the larger majority of Presbyterians who think about it conclude that God, who is not limited even to specific words, speaks through the English as well as the Hebrew and Greek translations of the Bible. His word is contained in the books of the Bible, which is completely and fully inspired even though the wording in the synoptic Gospels for instance, often differ. The truth of God is the same even though it is stated differently by different writers in different times. This view provides for *full inspiration* without a dictation theory in which it is asserted that men transcribed words and letters that meant nothing to them.

The reason why Presbyterians sometimes state their view of inspiration differently is that they interpret the meaning of the Catechism statement differently. Some people are so unsure that they take an extreme position and argue about it incessantly. Others are so sure that God speaks authoritatively through the scriptures that they are willing to allow for some difference in interpretation without surrendering their fundamental position. The Confession itself is strong without being rigid. It is very Presbyterian.

Since many students experience great doubts as they try to harmonize a view of inspiration with the findings of historical and literary criticism, a word might be said by the writer even though it is not said in the Presbyterian Standards. It is that Christians should never be afraid of the truth, but should be careful that they possess truth before accepting all opinions advanced. One may hold, for instance, to the full inspiration of the Pentateuch without being sure whether there are one, two, or ten authors; or one, two, three or more major sources. In the New Testament, Luke suggests that he uses several sources, yet he wrote one Gospel. Just as a cake is more than the sum of the ingredients used in making it, so the finished Bible is more than its parts. God could have inspired a writer or writers to select, edit and interpret materials so that they made Him known to man just as surely as He could have inspired a single man to write without reference to sources. To some Presbyterians whether He inspired Moses or a group of consecrated scholars

[27]

to write the Pentateuch is a matter of fact and not a matter of faith. To others the belief in the Mosaic authorship is a matter of faith. Whether or not we have an inspired Bible is a matter of faith to all. Let us continue to search for facts without destroying faith when facts are brought to light. Pin faith on truth that is revealed and it will never be shaken. But distinguish between opinion about possible human authors and faith in a God who speaks with authority through the Bible.

C. THE BIBLE IS OUR RULE OF FAITH AND LIFE

This leads us to the question of *authority*. According to the Roman Catholic church, the Bible is as authoritative as the church lets it become, and it is authoritative because the church makes it so. The Presbyterian belief is that the Bible is authoritative because God speaks through it. His authority is recognized by the believer, not only in the beauty and order and character of the Bible, but also because he has the *Amen* of the Holy Spirit within his heart. While this is true of many individuals, it becomes accumulative so that it may be said that the church as a whole has held to the Bible because it has found God speaking through it with a word of authority. Nothing can be said to equal the statements of our Confession in Chapter I, Article IV and V:

"The authority of the Holy Scripture, for which it ought to be believed and obeyed, dependeth not upon the testimony of any man or church, but wholly upon God (who is truth itself), the author thereof; and therefore it is to be received, because it is the word of God. "We may be moved and induced by the testimony of the church to an high and reverent esteem for the Holy Scripture; and the heavenliness of the matter, the efficacy of the doctrine, the majesty of the style, the consent of all the parts, the scope of the whole, (which is to give all glory to God), the full discovery it makes of the only way of man's salvation, the many other incomparable excellencies, and the entire perfection thereof, are arguments whereby it doth abundantly evidence itself to be the word of God; yet, notwithstanding, our full persuasion and assurance of the infallible truth and divine authority thereof, is from the inward work of the Holy Spirit, bearing witness by and with the word in our hearts."

D. THE BIBLE MUST BE PROPERLY INTERPRETED AND PUT TO WORK

Presbyterians believe that it is not enough to know that God has spoken an authoritative word to be obeyed by them. They must also learn to discover what God has said to others and what God is saying to them. For they know that the truth by which they must live is the truth they have found in the Bible. Since they do not accept the word of

[28]

some pope as to what the Bible means, they look to the Spirit of God to illuminate their minds as they read. They do not try to find all of science or history in the Bible. They do believe that it contains all that is necessary for God's glory, for man's salvation, for their faith and life. In order that the experience which produced the scriptures may be re-created in them, they follow the best principles of interpretation they can discover. Some of these, in the mind of the writer of these lessons, are as follows:

1. Read the Bible expectantly and prayerfully, listening for God to speak directly to your mind and heart.

2. Read a difficult passage several times and in several translations if you do not know how to use the original languages.

3. Study the historical background out of which the passage comes.

4. Study the context carefully. How does this verse fit into the paragraph, and how does the paragraph fit into the chapter and the book as a whole.

5. Compare other passages of scripture dealing with the same topic or theme. This is what our Standards mean by interpreting scripture by scripture.

6. Use reference books and commentaries for help in determining the meaning of a given passage.

7. Put all the truth you can to work right where you live. Fresh light often comes after the truth of God is tested in experience.

What all of this means is that Presbyterians know that it is not enough to hold a high view of inspiration concerning the writing of the Bible. They believe that it is a book to be obeyed, and that it points to a God who is to be obeyed in faith. It points to a Saviour who invites the response of the whole man.

When therefore we say we believe in the Bible, we do so without apology to any man. It has stood the test of time. It has been misinterpreted often by its friends and criticized by its foes. But always God speaks through it to call men to Himself. It reveals the life of God at work among the sons of men. It challenges us to let God come to life among us as we put its message to work in the twentieth century.

WORKSHEET

1. In the previous lesson we learned:
   a.
   b.
   c.

2. Our only rule of faith and life is the_____.

3. By revelation we mean that_____

   _____.

4. We believe that the Bible is an inspired record of_____

   _____of Himself to men.

5. The word inspired means_____ _____. God has inspired

   men at sundry_____and in divers_____.

6. There is an unchanging God, but there is also a_____
   understanding of God's will revealed in the scriptures.

7. We believe that inspiration extends to the_____of
   God's truth through the Hebrew and Greek languages, and our own
   language.

8. We believe that God guided in the_____and the

   _____of the books of the Bible.

9. We believe in the authority of the Bible, not because some pope or

   council says so, but because God by His_____
   authenticates the Bible in our hearts.

10. Because this experience of God speaking with authority through the
    Bible to many people in many centuries, we know that this is a

    _____as well as an individual experience.

11. Presbyterians believe that the Bible should be properly_____
    and put to work where people live. Some suggestions are made
    which will help to accomplish this purpose.

CHAPTER III

Our Sovereign God

INTRODUCTION

"Do PRESBYTERIANS still believe in the one-sided dogma of predestination?" So asks many an inquiring person, revealing that he understands neither Presbyterianism nor predestination.

The question, however, is natural and proper to ask even though it might not be asked in a way that pre-judges the case. For materialism has worked its subtle way into modern life through business attitudes and practices, the daily press, television, movies, radio, novels and plays to an extent where even earnest Presbyterians are hardly aware of the many impressions that come to them. And since so often the Christian churches have been slow to make their position clear, we need not be surprised that their members reflect their total impressions about life when they come to consider many theological questions.

Let us recognize at the outset that the doctrine of the sovereignty of God is a key Presbyterian doctrine. It is not, as will be shown in this chapter, either an irrelevant or a one-sided doctrine. Because of the many other points of view held by modern men, it may be helpful to distinguish the Presbyterian view of God's sovereignty from other points of view on the same topic.

A. VIEWS OF THE UNIVERSE THAT REJECT A SOVEREIGN GOD

Let us imagine for a moment that four college or university students are talking with their minister about Presbyterian beliefs.

1. NATURALISM

One of these students, whom we will call Jim, said: "I simply cannot accept the old-fashioned view that God created the world in seven days."

When asked by the minister what he can accept, the student replied: "I can accept the world of nature with its purpose, its relentless laws, its cruelty and its beauty. I believe that what is natural is right and should be followed in all of our relationships. I cannot fit into my view the Genesis story of creation and other stories in the Bible which describe a personal God as Lord of the universe. I live by my reason. I cannot see all of this business about faith in God as the church seems to teach."

The minister smiled and asked the young man: "Did you not say that you believe in a world of nature? Can you prove that the world of nature is the only kind of world there is? And when you talk about the natural being right, do you think of the natural as that represented by a beast satisfying its desires, or do you mean the sacrifices of a mother for her child? Do you not have a faith just as surely as the person who believes in a creator?"

The young man was somewhat flustered. It had not occurred to him either that he had accepted a world view on faith, or that it needed any defense. He hesitated and his minister continued:

"The point of view you express, even though it is very popular today, is not new. It is almost as old as civilization itself. Philosophers call it *naturalism*. Its basic and unproved assumption may be stated in three words: 'Nature is all.' These words may be reversed to say, 'All is nature.' Anyone who accepts this starting point for thought will find it impossible to believe that God is sovereign or that all of life should be related to His will.

"One of the reasons why Christianity is unalterably opposed to communism is that communism starts from a naturalistic and materialistic assumption. *Communists* assert that we live in a naturalistic world where all of life is a struggle between those who have material possessions and those who do not have them. In such a materialistic world it becomes the duty of those who lack to join together and take away from those who have. Since they are not responsible to any moral order or to any God above the universe (of whom they rid themselves by denying His existence), they use any method — cheating, lying, or killing — which furthers their ends. Actually they obey the dictates of a few party officials, but they do not often emphasize this fact. Their view of the world and of moral responsibility falls within the basic assumption that the universe is a naturalistic universe in which this struggle for control of material possessions is the only struggle that matters.

"American materialists may be mortal enemies of communism, not because they have a different basic assumption, but because they prefer their own advantage gained in a free-enterprise rather than a state-controlled system. They may exploit either labor or capital to selfish ends without any sense of responsibility to society or to God. Corruption in private business or in public life give ample evidence that materialism, while different from communism in Russia, stems from the soil of naturalism in philosophy. This does not mean that men and women who earn a living in the workaday world are all materialists. It is one thing to deal with material things, and quite another to believe that they are all that matter in one's world.

"Christianity differs with both communism and materialism because it holds that nature is not all and that materialism is not all there is to

[32]

life. The creator keeps watch over the world He has made and works His will in it.

"Modern pragmatism in thought, in economic life and in education, which seeks to achieve a social ideal without reference to a sovereign God, is another form of naturalism. It asserts that we live in a world of change (within a naturalistic universe) in which not even God can be accepted as an absolute. By experimentation men discover what is true or right for them in a given situation. All moral principles are relative rather than absolute. That is to say, no particular attitude or habit is right or wrong within itself. One attitude or habit may prove to be better in a given situation than another. This view of life is concerned with persons in themselves, not persons as creatures of God.

"You may have heard on your campus the words, 'Man is the measure of all things.' This humanistic dictum is borrowed from an ancient philosopher named Protagoras. It appeals to the ego of man. It allows men to decide matters of supreme importance without reference to any established truth or any sovereign God.

"You have doubtless detected a certain kinship between communism, materialism, pragmatism and humanism. While they differ in some respects, they all find their root in the assumption that nature is all and that there is no moral responsibility to any God above or beyond nature. This point of view might be illustrated with a closed circle in which you would find the words, 'Nature is all.' "

2. PANTHEISM

At this point in the minister's discourse, Jane, another of the four students, entered the conversation: "I certainly am glad to get some of these things out into the open. I must confess, however, that while I do not agree with Jim, I am inclined to agree with Somerset Maugham's philosophy which appeared in the picture, *The Razor's Edge,* a few years ago. In this picture a young man named Larry spent several years searching for God. He went all the way to India to talk with a holy man. One day he found God in a sunrise experience. I do not believe God should be thought of as a personal being, but as a spiritual force in the universe. This force, I believe, may be discovered at times by those who make a diligent search as Larry did."

When she had finished the minister asked, "At what point in his search did Larry turn to his Bible or go to the church around the corner?"

Jane sat with a puzzled look on her face for a moment. Then she said, "Come to think of it, I don't believe he ever did. I had not thought of that."

The minister continued: "The reason why Larry went neither to the Bible nor to the church is that the writer who created the character sought to avoid any reference to these sources. Why? Because his own view of the universe, as evidenced in his writings, does not recognize a God above or beyond the natural world, but a spiritual force within it. This ancient view, which has many other modern supporters, goes back at least to Buddha in the sixth century B.C. While the Buddha's views are not entirely clear to us, they may properly be designated as a form of *pantheism*. The fundamental proposition of pantheism is that "Everything is God; God is everything." When confined within the world of nature, this means that God is nature and nature is God.

"You may properly ask, What difference does it make to a Christian whether or not he accepts this view of the universe? We cannot give all the answers here, but let us mention a few. Pantheism rules out a personal God as a being above and beyond the universe. Such a God cannot be known easily in personal experience, as is well illustrated in the many years of search spent by Larry in *The Razor's Edge*. Such a God could not take human form in the Person of Jesus Christ. Such a God could not provide life beyond the earth. He might provide for the transmigration of one's soul to some other kind of earthly body. While the identity of the individual is not lost on this earth, there is a tendency toward losing personality in humanity or in the "world-soul" of the universe.

"Why do some people prefer this kind of view to Christianity? We cannot know all of the reasons. We may guess that some would like to be religious without having to discipline themselves to the ethics of Christianity. They find it hard intellectually to accept the doctrines of the Christian faith. It seems more defensible to keep the intellect working in a naturalistic world and to push religion into the realm of the intuition or the emotions. They do not seem to realize that they accept a view of the world in faith while trying to avoid that necessity in Christianity."

3. DEISM

Tom had been listening intently to all that was being said. He now contributed his pet idea to the discussion. "I think I agree with you that the points of view we have rejected are wrong. I am very much inclined to believe that there is a personal God who created the universe and put his moral laws within it. However, I cannot accept the miracles of the Bible or the idea of an incarnation of God in the flesh. For I do not believe God can invade the universe that He has created."

The minister responded: "The point of view you express is a product of thought which received its classic statement by John Locke (1632-

1704). Locke's famous *Essay Concerning Human Understanding* and other writings set forth his views. A popular illustration of deism, to which Locke gave philosophic expression, is the statement that God created the world, put His moral law within it, wound it up like a clock, and left it to run henceforth for itself. At no time could God re-enter the universe that He had created.

If you were to accept this kind of world, and if you tried to take on certain Christian assumptions, you would find yourself in conflict. For instance, deism would deny the possibility of miracles, of an incarnation of God in the flesh, the meaning of prayer, the effectiveness of the atonement, and many other doctrines of our religion. If you were to start with the deistic assumptions, you might believe that Jesus followed His views to His death, but you would lack the experience of receiving and using the power of the Holy Spirit."

Sue, the fourth student in the quartet, had listened to all of the preceding conversation with keen interest. She said: "I have tried to say some of these things to my friends, but I have not been able to state my Christian views very clearly. Could you state the Christian point of view as you have described these other points of view?"

"I will try", answered the minister. "Let us call it the Biblical point of view. Without putting it in quotes, I will tell you some of the things that Presbyterians believe about God and the universe. I will also try to help you understand predestination and human freedom in this universe as these doctrines are set forth in the Presbyterian Standards."

B. THE BIBLICAL POINT OF VIEW

Presbyterians start with the Biblical point of view that God is sovereign. This is in a real sense the key to all Presbyterian thought about God. They get this point of view from the Bible, which says, "In the beginning God. . ." in the very first book and "I am the alpha and the omega," (the beginning and the end) in the last book in our present arrangement.

The sovereignty of God may be presented under two basic Presbyterian doctrines. The first of these is that God is the creator of all things. The second is that God is the preserver of the universe, the One who is constantly acting to continue His creative activity and to hold all things in their proper order.

1. THE CREATOR OF THE UNIVERSE

Presbyterians believe in a created universe. The Hebrew text of Genesis 1:1 indicates that God created out of nothing the heavens and the earth. In the remainder of this epic story, it is indicated that He took this original matter and fashioned the universe as we know it in successive periods of time. Even though the sun and moon were not created until the fourth such period of time, these periods are called days. This does not necessarily mean that they were all equal or that they were all twenty-four hours in length. It does mean that at every stage of the creative process God was at work. This is to say that God could have created the world in six days of twenty-four hours each. But it is not to say that any facts about the length of the creative process which comes from other sources than the Bible would nullify the Genesis account of creation. Whether or not God is the creator is a matter of faith. Whether the days referred to in Genesis 1 are twenty-four hours each (especially with no sun or moon until the fourth period of time) becomes a matter of fact for reverent students of the Bible to discover. Some Presbyterians may believe in six days of twenty-four hours each as the period of creation. Some others may believe in six days of much longer duration, running into centuries. They agree in accepting the Theistic account of the origin of the world as this is given in the book of Genesis. And they agree that the crowning act of God's creation is man, who was made in the moral and spiritual image of God.

Because we know that God created all things for His own glory, we also recognize the fact that the creative activity of God continues through the ages. Every child who is born is looked upon by reverent parents as a sacred gift and trust from God. Every bird or animal or fish comes into existence through the creative activity of God as He works in the wonderful powers of nature which He has ordained. The researches of microscopes and telescopes magnify the glory seen with the naked eye to make us join the psalmist in exclaiming: "When I look at thy heavens, the work of thy fingers, the moon and the stars which thou hast established; what is man that thou art mindful of him, and the son of man that thou dost care for him?"* Because God is the creator and because He is acting constantly through the natural world that He has created, we are moved to recognize His sovereignty and His redemptive purpose in our lives.

2. THE ACTOR IN THE UNIVERSE

Presbyterians believe that God acts also in preserving the universe that He has created. The answer to Question 18 of the Larger Catechism states this doctrine in these words:

_____
*Psalm 8:3, 4. Unless otherwise indicated, all Bible quotations are from the Revised Standard Version, copyrighted by the National Council of Churches.

"God's works of providence are his most holy, wise, and powerful preserving, and governing all his creatures; ordering them, and all their actions, to his own glory."

Thus God acts according to His own character to uphold both His moral law and His eternal purpose in the experience of men and nations. While He ordinarily uses means to this end, He is not limited by natural means. God is Lord of history. God is Lord of nature. God is Lord of men whether or not they obey in faith, for He overrules their disobedience just as He honors their obedience.

This view of God as the creator and actor in the universe may be represented by a broken line drawn in a circle, above which is written, "God as Creator and Preserver of the Universe" and within which is written the words indicated below.

GOD AS CREATOR AND PRESERVER
REVEALED

1. In Nature

2. In history
   a. Jesus Christ
   b. Scriptures
   c. Church
   d. World movements

3. In individual
   experience

It should be noted that the Biblical view of creation, of miracles, of God's redemptive acts among men, of the incarnation, of the atonement, of future life all fit into this Theistic view of the universe. When seen from this point of view the great doctrines of our religion make sense.

Does not this view have its problems? Yes, it does. But it gives more satisfactory answers to life than does any other view. If one of you should ask, for instance, "Why is my friend crippled?", or "Why do we have floods and tornadoes that destroy innocent people?", we might give several partial answers to your questions.

First, we would recognize the fact that we sometimes contract diseases and experience illness of body because we fail to understand fully the laws of physical health. Our lack of understanding challenges doctors to attempt to discover what causes certain diseases, and to find ways that drugs and treatment may speed up physical recovery. God permits this process of nature to go on for the greatest good of the largest

[37]

number of people. Suppose, for instance, that immoral relations between the sexes had no unwholesome consequences. This would encourage rather than discourage such relations. For the sake of husbands and wives, for the sake of unborn children, nature brings consequences that teach the importance of social self-discipline.

Again, we reply concerning tornadoes and floods that God ordinarily works through the laws of nature. When men destroy their forests, they may invite the winds to sweep across the plains. When they build their houses beside the river bed, they risk the dangers of a flood. Yet we know that without the wind, the flowers and trees could not pollinate properly. And without the water from the river, people would not have sufficient water for themselves, their stock or their crops. By the laws of nature an apple drops to the ground where it may be picked up and used. By the law of gravity a person falls from a building. But by the same law he is able to walk, to ride in a car, to do the dozens of things on which his life depends. It is therefore not surprising that our Confession of Faith, recognizing God as the first Cause of all things, also adds: "Yet, by the same providence, he ordereth them to fall out according to the nature of second causes, either necessarily, freely, or contingently." (Chapter V, Article II).

In similar fashion the moral choices of man have consequences that drive them away from God or draw them closer to God. While God is free to work "without, above, and against" the means He has set up, He ordinarily works with men who make free choices in a moral world. Such a world, where evil choices are possible, is the best world for the largest number. If spiritual blessedness flowed directly from evil choices and habits, there would be little possibility of encouraging anyone to seek the will of God. Even though believers sometimes suffer, this suffering may well become a means of spiritual growth.

No better illustration of the wisdom and the providence of God can be cited than that of Jesus who suffered, died, and was raised by the power of God. While He was suffering, it seemed that God had permitted a terrible mistake to occur. Yet because of who He was, and because of what He did, the consequences of the crucifixion of Jesus have come across many centuries to us. The release of God's redemptive power through the crucified and risen Lord did not seem very apparent during the trial and crucifixion of Jesus. Yet because God is Lord of history, and because God's purpose will ultimately be accomplished either through the opposition of men or through the consecrated obedience of men, Jesus' death and resurrection have had and still have tremendous redemptive power. In the sphere of history and in the sphere of human experience, the final ordering is the Lord's.

C. PREDESTINATION AND HUMAN FREEDOM IN GOD'S UNIVERSE

We cannot give adequate treatment to either of these ideas, but we may point in the direction which leads to truth. Further statement will be found in the Confession of Faith under the topics of the decrees of God and of free will. Let us begin by stating that Presbyterians believe in predestination. Let us state what predestination is *not* so that we may better understand what it *is*.

1. PREDESTINATION

First, predestination is not fatalism. Fatalism has classic expression in two historic forms. One is that represented by Mohammedans who accept good and ill, wickedness and righteousness as the will of God. While they do not completely deny human responsibility, they are taught to say repeatedly, "It is the will of Allah; praised be Allah." The extreme minimizing of human responsibility produces at best a very limited moral growth. This point of view is not predestination, but fatalism.

Another form of fatalism is the modern philosophic form called determinism. Determinism has many forms, but tends to be related to a naturalistic rather than a Theistic universe. While giving more or less emphasis to secondary causes, determinism points to a succession of events and reactions which predetermine the result. What is to be will be in determinism. Therefore to pray to a God above the universe or to feel responsible to such a God is to miss the determinism of the world in which one lives. Again we suggest that this is fatalism and not predestination.

Then what is predestination? The three basic articles on which el. boration is made in the Confession are as follows:

I   "God from all eternity did by the most wise and holy counsel of his own will, freely and unchangeably ordain whatsoever comes to pass; yet so as thereby neither is God the author of sin; nor is violence offered to the will of the creatures, nor is the liberty or contingency of second causes taken away, but rather established.

II "Although God knows whatsoever may or can come to pass, upon all supposed conditions; yet hath he not decreed anything because he foresaw it as future, or as that which would come to pass, upon such conditions.

III "By the decree of God, for the manifestation of his glory, some men and angels are predestinated unto everlasting life, and others fore-ordained to everlasting death." (Chapter III, Articles I, II, III.)

Let us recognize the fact that the starting point for predestination is the eternal purpose of a sovereign God. This God is a God of love and righteousness. He is a God of holiness and wisdom. The character of God is important, for it determines the nature of His decrees. And these decrees are both for God's glory and man's greatest good. They initiate whatever comes to pass either directly or indirectly.

A second point is that God is not the author of sin. He created a world in which sin was possible through the wrong choices of moral agents. He permitted man's freedom to choose, as we shall see more fully in a few moments. But it is both short-sighted and irreverent to blame God for the sins that we think up for ourselves.

A third point is that man's freedom is not taken away. While it is fully recognized that, through the fall, man has lost his fellowship with God and his desire to do the will of God, man is yet free to choose whether or not he will respond to God's revelation and God's grace in the Gospel.

A fourth point is that second causes are not taken away by God's decrees. The consequences of choices, of actions and of habits do come to men. David sinned against Uriah and took his wife. The child born to David and Bathsheba died. Absalom almost usurped David's kingdom. Solomon magnified the weakness of David and developed a harem. Rehoboam, desiring to inherit the harem, decided to keep high taxes and thus split the kingdom. David was forgiven after he sought pardon from God. He was sustained and strengthened in his suffering, but the consequences of his sin followed in the lives of his descendents. This is an illustration of the fact that God does not take away, but rather establish the secondary causes which have their effects in the lives of men.

A fifth point is that predestination does not depend on foreknowledge. God has foreknowledge, to be sure. But His purpose is primary. That comes first. If His purpose depended on foreknowledge of what any given person or group of persons would do, it would leave the final word in the universe to man and not to God. Man rather than God would be sovereign. While therefore God foreknows what men will do, and while He does not destroy their freedom to choose, God ultimately rules and overrules to accomplish His purpose. The case of the Hebrews who refused to go into Canaan and of the new generation which finally did illustrates how God accomplished His purpose to lead the Hebrews into the Land of Promise. If the purpose had been left to the Hebrews, it is very doubtful whether they would ever have gone into Canaan. Martin Luther, John Calvin, John Knox, and a host of other Christians have rendered their service, not because of their own will, but because they responded to God's will for them from eternity. This is therefore a challenging and important aspect of predestination.

A sixth point is that predestination extends to both the saved and the damned for eternity. As will be seen in a later chapter, the sin of man since the fall leaves him utterly incapable of desiring or achieving salvation for himself. Some by the decree of God and by their own will, are left to suffer the consequences of their own sin. Others, by the mercy of God, are elected unto salvation. No one who responds to the Gospel is denied salvation. It is recognized that man has neither the mind nor the ability to understand how God thus works in redemptive love. The believer is therefore urged (See Chapter III, Article VIII), to handle this high mystery of predestination with special prudence and care. In the doctrine concerning the Gospel it is stated:

"In the gospel God declares his love for the world and his desire that all men should be saved; reveals fully and clearly the only way of salvation; promises eternal life to all who truly repent and believe in Christ; invites and commands all to embrace the offered mercy; and by His Spirit accompanying the word pleads with men to accept his gracious invitation." (Chapter X, Article II).

Let it be made unmistakably clear that no person who desires the experience of a saving knowledge of Jesus Christ is denied such an experience. God does not act out of His own character, which is a character of holiness, righteousness and love. The appended statement at the end of this chapter occurs in the Confession of Faith used by the United Presbyterian Church, U.S.A., and is an effort to clarify the present understanding of certain inferences that have been drawn from the Confession. It is given as information for members of that branch of Presbyterianism and not as a part of the Confession of Faith as used by the Presbyterian Church, U.S.

2. Human Freedom and Responsibility

It would be most unfair to present God's sovereignty in human affairs without also recognizing man's freedom and responsibility. For this is the other side of the coin, as it were, which helps us to image the whole. Let us state briefly a few of the things Presbyterians believe about human freedom.

First, the freedom of man's will is created by God. Chapter XI, Article I of the Confession of Faith states the position in this fashion:

"God hath endued the will of man with that natural liberty, that it is neither forced, nor by any absolute necessity of nature determined to good or evil."

[41]

This is to say that one chooses freely to do one thing or another. One chooses to cross a street or not to cross it. One may choose to obey the law of gravity or to disobey it. One may choose to attend the church service or to stay at home. One may choose in his personal or social habits to be Christian or less than Christian. All of this we know by experience and by the teachings of scripture.

Second, the power of man's choice is not absolute. We do not think with our minds alone or decide with our wills alone. As human beings we are made so that we are one whole. At any given moment we think with both the conscious and the sub-conscious layers (sometimes perhaps the unconscious layers) of our minds. Previous emotional and psychological experiences create favorable or unfavorable responses to ideas so that no one of us thinks objectively or independently. The reason why it is harder for older persons to become Christians than for younger persons is that older persons have already formed attitudes and habits which tend to prevent good choices. Both original weakness and actual sins make it impossible to think and act freely. More will be said about the effects of sin in human personality in a later chapter. Suffice it to say here that our power of choice is influenced greatly by previous experiences, and is never absolute.

Third, God provides His grace to free man from his bondage so that he may will to do what is spiritually good. Thus man is enabled to respond to God's revelation in the scriptures and in Jesus Christ. So Jesus said: "All that the Father gives me will come to me; and him who comes to me I will not cast out." (John 6:37).

Fourth, the choices that men make with their freedom have moral and spiritual consequences. God ordinarily works through our choices, not apart from them. When the Pharaoh of Egypt repeatedly hardened his heart, or when God hardened his heart by offering him choices (See Exodus 5-11), he acted freely. But each wrong choice made a right choice harder to make. And the final result was the loss of the Hebrew slaves which was the Pharaoh's purpose to prevent.

Likewise Jesus said concerning Judas: "For the Son of man goes as it has been determined; but woe to that man by whom he is betrayed!" (Luke 22:22). How God would have worked out the arrest of Jesus without Judas' betrayal is something we do not know. But we do know that Judas was held responsible for his act and that he committed suicide.

We are free to choose, therefore, to reject Christ or to commit ourselves to Him day by day. The consequences of rejection will be a life without God, and of commitment will be a rich life with God. Neither the scriptures nor Presbyterian doctrine deny to man human freedom or responsibility for his choices.

[42]

Since we have given a brief summary of these two points of view, you doubtless ask how divine predestination and human freedom can be harmonized with one another. They have never been completely harmonized in systematic theology. Yet in Christian experience we know at least partially how they overlap and interfuse. When we pray as though everything depends on God and work as though everything depends on us we learn something of how God and man work together. A paraphrase of Philippians 2:12b, 13, which brings out its meaning, would be: "Keep on working out your own salvation with fear and trembling, for it is God who is constantly at work within you, both to guide and enable your will, and to accomplish His will in your life." Oftentimes we are not aware of God's working until occasionally we look back on our experience to see how a series of choices has led us to a larger and richer understanding of the will of God.

We therefore conclude that predestination does not destroy human freedom. It is not fatalism in thought. It does not lead to moral weakness in conduct. It rather provides a challenge to commit ourselves wholly to God; to recognize that we live and move and have our being in the purpose of God; that we have a divinely appointed mission in the world, that we are free to choose God's will for ourselves; and that, by God's grace and power, we are enabled to achieve that will in His name. It is a high mystery. But it is a strong doctrine which produces prophets and apostles, ministers and lay persons who live with a sense of deep stewardship and high partnership with God. Presbyterians are not ashamed to say that they believe in the sovereignty of God, in divine predestination and human freedom.

DECLARATORY STATEMENT

While the ordination vow of ministers, ruling elders, and deacons, as set forth in the Form of Government, requires the reception and adoption of the Confession of Faith only as containing the System of Doctrine taught in the Holy Scriptures, nevertheless, seeing that the desire has been formally expressed for a disavowal by the Church of certain inferences drawn from statements in the Confession of Faith, and also for a declaration of certain aspects of revealed truth which appear at the present time to call for more explicit statement, therefore the Presbyterian Church in the United States of America does authoritatively declare as follows:

FIRST, with reference to Chapter III of the Confession of Faith: that concerning those who are saved in Christ, the doctrine of God's eternal decree is held in harmony with the doctrine of his love to all mankind, his gift of his Son to be the propitiation for the sins of the world, and his readiness to bestow his saving grace to all who seek it.

That concerning those who perish, the doctrine of God's eternal decree is held in harmony with the doctrine that God desires not the death of any sinner, but has provided in Christ a salvation sufficient for all, adapted to all, and freely offered in the gospel to all; that men are fully responsible for their treatment of God's gracious offer; that his decree hinders no man from accepting that offer; and that no man is condemned except on the ground of his sin.

SECOND, With reference to Chapter X, Section III, of the Confession of Faith, that is not to be regarded as teaching that any who die in infancy are lost. We believe that all dying in infancy are included in the election of grace, and are regenerated and saved by the Christ through the Spirit, who works when and where and how he pleases.

(Quoted from Standards of U.P.-U.S.A. Church.)

WORKSHEET

1. The three world views that reject the idea of a sovereign God are:

   a. The_____, which holds_____.

   b. The_____, which holds_____.

   c. The_____, which holds_____.

2. I cannot fully accept any of the above points of view because:

   a.

   b.

3. The biblical point of view is that God is_____and_____ of the universe.

4. This point of view recognizes that God reveals Himself:

   a. In_____.

   b. In history, including the revelation in_____,

   _____ the_____and in_____

   _____.

5. Presbyterians believe in predestination. Predestination is not_____

   _____, but is a view of the world which begins with God's eternal purpose or decree.

6. Six points were made concerning predestination. These are:

b.

c.

d.

e.

f.

7. **Four points were made concerning human freedom and responsibility:**

    a.

    b.

    c.

    d.

CHAPTER IV

Our Triune God

INTRODUCTION

Since each of these chapters carries forward the thought of those that precede, let us review briefly the preceding chapter. In it we considered the sovereignty of God, interpreted in the scriptures, as the keystone to all Presbyterian thought. We recognized other points of view and the Biblical point of view. Then we presented God as the creator and preserver of the universe, and attempted to understand predestination and human freedom in God's universe. Now we turn to recognize the difficulty of understanding the Trinity, then the meaning of the Trinity, the functions of the three Persons in the God-head, and the difference the Trinity makes to believers.

A. THE DIFFICULTY OF UNDERSTANDING THE TRINITY

Two adolescent girls, one of them a Jew and the other a Christian, were good friends at school. One day they began to talk about God. They agreed that they both worshiped a God who could not be seen with physical eyes, who always existed, who had all wisdom and power, and who was concerned about His creatures on the earth. But when they came to the number of Persons in the God-head, they began to differ.

The Jewish girl said: "We worship one God only. The Lord our God is one. We do not worship three Gods as you Christians do."

The Christian girl said: "We worship one God only. But we worship God who has revealed Himself as Father, as Son, and as Holy Spirit."

Because she did not understand her belief about the Trinity very well, she found it hard to present that belief to her friend. But her problem is not peculiar to youth. Theologians in different centuries have puzzled over, and have sometimes modified the doctrine of the Trinity to suit their own understanding of God.

Take, for example, the belief of the Greek Orthodox church. The accepted creedal position, which was arrived at in controversy with the Western church, is that the Holy Spirit proceeds from the Father but not from the Son. The deity of the Son is not denied, but He is not believed to have been sufficiently equal with the Father to participate in sending the Holy Spirit. Without going into the theological arguments, we may recognize in this belief a modification of the doctrine of the Trinity as held by the Western church and the major branches of Protantism.

An example of the outright rejection of the doctrine of the Trinity is to be found in the teaching of the Unitarian church. In this teaching Jesus is presented as the best man who has ever lived, and as the perfect example for humanity. He lived closer to God than anyone else has lived. He dared to die for his faith. The Spirit of God is an expression of God and a power of God which is known in human experience, but is not the power of the Holy Spirit in the traditional Christian sense. Unitarianism, because of its rejection of the Bible as its final authority, and because of its free spirit, has modified its own teachings to a point where no official body of doctrine exists. But it does agree in principle to a rejection of the Trinity.

Of these three classic types of theology, the Greek Orthodox modifies somewhat, and the Jewish and Unitarian faiths deny outright the doctrine of the Trinity. Presbyterians may properly ask, What do we believe about the Trinity? How may we give answer to our friends who charge that we worship three Gods instead of one? Let us examine briefly what we mean by the Trinity.

B. THE MEANING OF THE TRINITY

It is not too much to assert that there is no single theologian in history who has ever been able fully to explain the Trinity. We know only in part. But our knowing in part does not prevent that partial knowledge from being accurate as far as it goes. When therefore as Presbyterians we affirm our belief in the Trinity, we follow the scriptures which present this great mystery. In answer to Question 6 of the Shorter Catechism we affirm: "There are three persons in the God-head: the Father, the Son, and the Holy Ghost; and these three are one God, the same in substance, equal in power and glory."

While it is true that we cannot explain the Trinity fully, we may approach the essential idea of three persons and one substance with an analogy from the world of science. If someone were to ask you, "What is H_2O?", you might quickly answer, "It is water, of course." When pressed further, you might modify your statement to say, "It is either ice, water, or steam, depending on the temperature." This latter statement would be more accurate than the first. For below freezing temperature, H_2O is ice and has all of the properties of ice. Above freezing and below evaporization temperature, H_2O is water, and has all of the properties of water. We use it in many forms in our daily life. Above vaporizing temperature H_2O is steam, having still other properties. One would not drink steam or attempt to pour it into a container. Yet by chemical analysis steam contains the same elements of Hydrogen and Oxygen that ice and water do. It is the same in substance.

[47]

This is not an explanation of the Trinity, but is an analogy which helps us to see how God as a spiritual being is revealed in scripture in three persons. The Larger Catechism, in answer to Question 7, asserts:

"God is a Spirit, in and of himself infinite in being, glory, blessedness, and perfection; all-sufficient, eternal, unchangeable, incomprehensible, everywhere present, almighty; knowing all things, most wise, most holy, most just, most merciful and gracious, longsuffering, and abundant in goodness and truth."

Each of these characteristics deserves meditation and consideration. They point to the character of God as Spirit and not as matter. He is spiritual Being in essence. He is in Himself all-sufficient and almighty. He is everywhere present. He knows all things. He is just, loving, and gracious. The qualities revealed in the Old Testament and the New belong to Him. In Himself and in all His attributes we believe that God is one.

At the same time we believe that God has revealed Himself in the scriptures in three ways: as Father, as Son, and as Holy Spirit. All three are personal revelations of the same God. To any who would question our belief we would say that the same God who spoke to Abraham, to Moses and the prophets also spoke through His Son incarnate in the flesh. It was Jesus Himself who said, near the end of His ministry, "He who has seen me has seen the Father" (John 14:9). Before He departed this life Jesus promised to return in the person of the Holy Spirit. The risen Christ who ascended to glory after His resurrection ministry of about forty days came in the person of the Holy Spirit upon the church at Pentecost. He has been coming ever since upon believers who were willing to receive Him. In Christian experience the apparent intellectual impossibility is resolved, and God is known as Father, Son, and Holy Spirit. Those who miss this high doctrine have also missed something very important in Christian experience. Therefore Presbyterians cannot surrender their belief in the Trinity even though some of their friends in other faiths may do so.

C. THE FUNCTIONS OF THE THREE PERSONS IN THE GOD-HEAD

The functions of the three persons of the Trinity are clearly outlined in Ephesians 1:4-14. Verses 4-6a present God the Father as electing saints in Christ and as adopting believers as sons. God chooses and ordains men for His own glory. He invites believers to view their redeemed life, not as the result of caprice or chance, but as a part of the purpose of the eternal God. This eternal purpose of God brings believers into a filial or father-child relationship with God. When two parents adopt a child, they claim that child for themselves and of their own free will give that child the love and care that they would have given a child born in their own family. The adopted child has the privileges and the inheritance of a child born in the family. Before the law the child is declared to be the same as if he were born to those parents. Thus the Father purposes to redeem His own and adopts them as sons.

The primary function of the Son is to provide the redemption which brings a believer into an experience of sonship to God. Verses 6b-12 describe the redemptive work of Christ in providing this redemption. Jesus Christ who gave His life for us redeems us by His blood. He not only forgives past sins, but also provides the power for the new way of life. When men looked into the face of Jesus Christ, when they saw His mighty works, when they heard His teachings, when they saw Him die on the cross, when they obeyed the instructions of the risen Lord, they came to know that God is gracious. The riches of God's grace belonged to those who believed. Christ made them a heritage through their faith in Him. That heritage was pointed toward in the covenant relationship in the Old Testament and made full of meaning in the New. For as Paul says in Romans 4 and 9, the spiritual seed of Abraham inherit the covenant promises of God. They find their destiny in their faithful obedience to the Son. They accept for themselves and for their children the redemption provided in the Son.

Not only do Presbyterians believe that the Father purposes the redemption which the Son provides, but they also believe that the primary function of the Holy Spirit is to apply this redemption to believers so as to make it operative in their daily living. The salvation of believers is an experience which begins at some moment in time but which continues throughout eternity. Redemption is provided once for all in Christ. It is applied continuously by the Holy Spirit. The Holy Spirit causes a believer to respond to God in faith. The Holy Spirit nurtures the child of faith in Christian growth. Just as the Holy Spirit united with the Virgin Mary to produce God's Son in the flesh, so the Holy Spirit unites with the heart of believers to reproduce Christ's life in them. The nickname given to believers in Antoich was more accurate than the critics knew. For the word Christian means "little Christ". It is ours to make the name as meaningful as they did.

Some people use the wrong pronoun to refer to the Holy Spirit. They refer to Him as "it". The New Testament does not follow this practice. No more should we. He is the third person of the Trinity. He would dwell in us and give us guidance and power. He would remake us into the likeness of Christ. He would make redemption, purposed by the Father and provided by the Son, operative in our lives.

[49]

D. THE DIFFERENCE THE TRINITY MAKES TO BELIEVERS

Both young and old may ask why it makes any difference whether or not we believe in the Trinity. We believe that question has been partially answered. It makes a great deal of difference to the believer that from the very beginning of God's purpose and plan for the world, his life has been significant. Because it is a part of God's plan, it can never become insignificant. Others may view themselves as flies on some giant millwheel in space revolving in a circle, but Presbyterians believe that God the Father has a purpose for their lives.

It also makes a difference that we can look into the face of Jesus Christ and know better what God is like. He was not known too well even in the experiences of Abraham, Moses, and the prophets. But He became very personal in the incarnate Son who provided redemption for believers. God showed Himself as a Friend and as a Saviour in His Son. It is good to know that the Redeemer of the universe is our Friend.

Because we know that the Holy Spirit moves us to believe and to grow in our faith, we respond with confidence to our great Ally. We cannot lift ourselves by our own bootstraps, but we can overcome our temptations by the indwelling power of the Holy Spirit. When we are in danger or darkness, we are encouraged by a consciousness of the fact that He is nearer than breathing. When we despair of our progress in the Gospel, He comforts us and spurs us on to new endeavor. He becomes in us the down-payment of our eternal life beyond the grave, for He brings the life and power of the living God into our hearts. By the power of the Triune God, we who seek the victory hereafter already know the life of victory here.

Presbyterians therefore do not hesitate to affirm their faith in the Trinity. Against the background of this great doctrine they move forward in thought to consider many other phases of their historic faith.

WORKSHEET

1. This chapter deals with the Trinity. By the Trinity we mean the unity

   of the_____, the_____, and the_____ as three persons, yet as one in essence.

2. The three classic types of theology which deny the reality of the Trinity are:

   a. The_____, which rejects the deity of Jesus Christ, and the procession of the Holy Spirit, affirming that God is one God only.

b. The _____, which affirms the reality of God the Father, God the Son, and God the Holy Spirit in a sense, but which rejects the idea that the Holy Spirit proceeds from the Son as well as from the Father.

The _____, which rejects the Trinity by rejecting the deity of Jesus Christ and hence also the New Testament idea that the Holy Spirit comes from the Father and the Son, that these three are one in substance.

3. The analogy from nature was suggested to point toward the truth of one God as Spirit in substance, yet revealed as Father, Son, and Holy Spirit. I found this analogy_____in thinking about the Trinity.

4. The Father_____man's redemption; the Son_____ redemption, and the Holy Spirit_____redemption to believers.

5. I believe the doctrine of the Trinity is helpful to me because:

   a.

   b.

   c.

6. I would like further discussion of the following topics:

   a.

   b.

[51]

CHAPTER V

Our Need of God's Redemption

INTRODUCTION

It is not at all unusual for someone to say to a Presbyterian, "I do not like your idea of the sinfulness of man. You make people feel like so many worms. And you try to make people good by telling them how bad they are. You discourage rather than encourage the achievement of goodness."

Some Presbyterians may be taken aback by such a charge. But those who have thought through their beliefs may well suggest that the taller the building, the deeper the foundation. We must be honest about man's sinfulness if we are to show men how to become righteous.

We should also clarify the point of view from which we begin our thinking. If we are merely comparing the goodness of one person with another, we may be optimistic about that person. But if we start with the viewpoint of the holy character of God, we may change our ideas. Black beside gray shows less contrast than does black beside white. Presbyterians begin their thinking about man's sin in the light of the holiness of God. But they do so only in order to lead men to the holiness of God. Let us therefore examine the meaning of the fall, the subtle and destructive power of sin, and the punishment which is due for sin.

A. THE MEANING OF THE FALL

Presbyterians recognize their need of redemption, not only because of their own sinful acts, but also because of a historic fall on the part of our first parents. Adam and Eve were created in an estate of holiness and happiness, but fell from their holiness by yielding to temptation and eating the forbidden fruit. Their sin may be defined as selfishness, as rebellion, and as disobedience. All of these and more are involved in their eating of the forbidden fruit.

Several questions come to our minds as we think about the sin of Adam and Eve. One is why a good God would permit this sin. Another is whether or not God is responsible for the evil that is in the world. A third is whether or not moral traits can be inherited. Before attempting to answer these questions, let us consider four possible kinds of worlds that might have been created.

1. THREE KINDS OF WORLD ARE UNSATISFACTORY

It is possible to conceive of a world in which there is no absolute authority over man. In such a world every man could do as he pleased.

This kind of world would lead to anarchy in thought and in conduct. It would lead (as it has time and again) to lying and cheating and killing, to all forms of dishonesty and pride. It would lead to a world in which no one could be trusted. This kind of world invites totalitarian dictatorship in which the strong oppress the weak and use them for their own purposes. In spite of all the evidences that point to this kind of world, Christians do not believe that it gives an adequate picture of the world in which they live.

It is possible also to conceive of a world in which there is absolute moral authority, in which God is responsible for every act of every person, and in which human beings are like puppets in a puppet show. God would move the strings and men would react. They would be automatons or machines or puppets. No moral choices would be made except by the God who manipulates the strings. Presbyterians do not believe that God made this kind of world.

A third possible world is a world where man sets up the organized authority at first and this authority perpetuates itself in the name of society. The authority may be primarily religious or political. It requires blind and unthinking obedience on the part of those over whom it is exercised. No matter what the teaching may be, if it is given in the name of the state or of the church, it must be obeyed. To disobey is to suffer discipline which may be very severe. Men must obey regardless of their own judgment or conscience about a given idea, dogma, or practice. The totalitarian representatives of this point of view are in our world and are at odds with one another. Both want to rule and to accomplish their own ends. They convince themselves that these ends justify the means used for their accomplishment. But Presbyterians do not believe that God created a world where the individual has no direct responsibility to Himself. They believe that while the religious authority exercised by the Roman church has some real values, it is not the kind of authority God intended or that Christ taught should be established.

2. The World of the Bible

The fourth kind of world, we believe, is revealed in the scriptures. It is a world in which, in order to provide for moral responsibility, man has freedom of choice within limits set by God. God created this world which in itself was not evil, but had in it the possibility of evil through the wrong choices of man. God permitted Adam and Eve to eat of all of the trees of the garden except one. He set limits on that one, not so much to make life hard for Adam and Eve as to permit them to grow through their faithful obedience. They assumed that their way was better for them than God's way for them. They yielded to temptation

[53]

and decided to disobey. They suffered in personality and in experience for their disobedience.

We cannot be certain why God permitted evil to come into the world. We can recognize the fact that anarchy or a puppet show or a self-perpetuating human authority tends to destroy moral freedom and moral responsibility. And man was made in the moral and spiritual image of God — capable of moral choices which would have good or evil consequences. We can therefore see the logical necessity for the possibility of evil if there was to be any human responsibility. To deny the choice of man is to remove his responsibility and to stunt his capacity for moral growth.

3. GOD IS NOT RESPONSIBLE FOR EVIL IN THE WORLD

In reply to the second question, "Is God responsible for the evil in the world?", we give a negative reply. God created a world where evil was possible through man's moral choice, but man himself chose to rebel and to disobey. Man brought the consequences on himself in a moral universe. God permitted this sin but did not decree it.

4. REASONS WHY MORAL CHOICES ARE IMPORTANT

If we should inquire, "Why are moral choices so important?" a ready answer offers itself. We make our choices and they in turn make us. A series of choices to resist God, like those made by the selfish Pharaoh of Egypt in Moses' time, hardens the personality and the will against God. A series of choices to obey God, as illustrated by Saul of Tarsus during and after his conversion, makes a person more responsive to God. We become better or worse through our moral choices. As we saw in the preceding chapter, while God is sovereign, men are free to choose.

5. THE SIGNIFICANCE OF THE FALL TO ADAM AND HIS POSTERITY

When we think of what the fall meant to Adam and Eve, we are led to realize that they had a consciousness of disobedience to God's moral law. This kind of disobedience is described in the Greek Version of the Old Testament with the word *anomia*. It means a breaking over, a transgression of a known law of God. The other consciousness that Adam and Eve had was a consciousness of having failed to measure up to the full will of God for their lives. In the same Version this experience is described with the word *harmartia*. Interestingly enough, the use of this word in the Greek Old Testament and in the New Testament is about three times as frequent as the use of *anomia*. The idea is well summarized in James 4:17: "Whoever knows what is right to do and fails to do it, for him it is sin."

[54]

Adam and Eve did not steal. They did not commit murder. They did not bear false witness against one another. They disobeyed God and they failed to measure up to their possibilities as creatures of God. Their moral choices led to the corruption of their whole selves. This corruption is referred to in our Confession of Faith as the fall from original innocence and grace to an estate of sin and misery.

The nature of this estate of sin and misery is described in the Larger Catechism, Answer to Question 25, in these words:

"The sinfulness of that estate whereinto man fell, consisteth in the guilt of Adam's first sin, the want of that righteousness wherein he was created, and the corruption of his nature, whereby he is utterly indisposed, disabled, and made opposite unto all that is spiritually good, and wholly inclined to all evil, and that continually; which is commonly called original sin, and from which do proceed all actual transgressions."

Observe the sense of guilt which drives the sinner away from happy fellowship with a righteous God. This sense of guilt led Adam and Eve to try to hide from God. But Adam became utterly indisposed to good, unable to achieve it in his life, and wholly inclined to continual evil.

The Presbyterian Standards describe the meaning of the fall to Adam's posterity in these words:

"Original sin is conveyed from our first parents unto their posterity by natural generation, so as all that proceed from them in that way, are conceived and born in sin." (Question 26, Larger Catechism)

This doctrine, which was debated in the time of Augustine and has been a matter of dispute ever since, recognizes the close relationship between the body and the personality of an individual. It takes human beings to be whole persons, not persons in isolation from their bodies. It recognizes the universality of sin among men. It sees human nature as sinful, not only in the sense of failing to measure up to the best that is possible, but also as acting contrary to God's holy will. Again we must keep the point of view suggested at the beginning of this chapter. Man is looked upon as sinful, not so much from man's point of view, but from God's point of view, which is one of complete holiness.

Someone will ask, "Do you mean to infer by this doctrine that I inherited my sinfulness from my saintly mother?" To this question we would reply that your saintly mother would probably be quick to recognize her sinfulness before God. It is her constant recognition of her own weakness and her constant laying hold on God's redemptive power which has made her saintly. She would be the first to tell you that she was not born a saint, but that she grew into whatever saintliness of character she has after her rebirth from above.

A second answer that she would likely give is that you must overcome the natural sinfulness you received through birth in the same way that she did. You cannot choose or desire the best in holiness without the help of the Spirit of God. Your very resistance to the fact of your own sinfulness is an evidence that, apart from the Holy Spirit, you would deal with your sin by denying its existence. And that is partly what you have received by natural generation.

A third answer she would give you is that while you are born in sin, you are also born with the possibility of responding to the Spirit of God. You cannot save yourself, but you may respond to the Spirit of God and be reborn from above. She would urge you to recognize this necessity. For while she may provide food and clothing, she cannot make you grow. You must grow physically and spiritually through your own exercise. She can transmit to you the possibility of growth, but you have to experience growth yourself. So you gain nothing by getting off into an academic debate about whether or not moral traits can be transmitted by physical generation. For moral traits cannot be separated from the persons who develop them. And even those who deny the possibility of transmitting moral traits must recognize the tendency of children to emulate the moral traits gained from parents whose example is transmitted unawares.

Persons who suffer from blindness of mind, strong delusions, hardness of heart, horror of conscience or vile affections (The Larger Catechism, Q. 28), may well concern themselves more to seek redemption from God than to deny their sin by denying the possibility of inheriting it.

Many Presbyterians will freely admit the difficulties associated with this doctrine, which is sometimes called the doctrine of total depravity. Yet they find clear indications in the scriptures that they deny their sin at their own peril. The fall means that mankind has within itself the seeds of its own destruction as well as the possibility of salvation for all who will commit themselves to God in Christ. Few parents with small children will deny the actual presence at times of the spirit of disobedience which dwells in all of us.

B. THE SUBTLE AND DESTRUCTIVE POWER OF SIN

The continuation of sin in man is described in the Confession in the following significant words:

"From this original corruption, whereby we are utterly indis-posed, disabled, and made opposite to all good, and wholly inclined to all evil, do proceed all actual transgressions.

"This corruption of nature, during this life, doth remain in those that are regenerated: and although it be through Christ pardoned and mortified, yet both itself, and all the motions thereof, are truly and properly sin." (Chapter VI, Articles IV and V)

1. THE DOWNWARD PATH OF MAN

Do these words mean that God deliberately and arbitrarily makes men suffer? Not at all. Men suffer the consequences of their actual transgressions because they get started on the downward path and lose their insight into what is right and what is wrong. The steps downward are well illustrated in Romans 1:18-32. Man's first step toward his self-destruction is his failure to see God in nature. This leads him to give up a Theistic view of the universe and inevitably to become vain in his reasoning. As a consequence his senseless heart is darkened. He cannot think clearly about God or about what is right or wrong.

The next step is to make nature his god. To be sure, he may single out some creature or some part of the creation as an object of wor-ship. Often materialism becomes king and men go mad with greed or power. A Hitler or a Stalin or a political party may take the place of God. In the name of such a god much havoc and evil have been wrought in the world. Innocent people have been caught up in the vortex of the flaming and destructive power of sin. Whether the form of material-ism is money or power or ambition, it destroys the very kind of life it tends to deify.

Then because men refuse to have God in their knowledge and be-cause they make some part of nature their god, they are given up to abuse their bodies. This they do with every vile passion which suggests itself to them. Like a descending spiral, they are led from the abuse of their bodies to the fourth stage of debasing their minds so that they think more like beasts than like men. This combination of vile passions and debased minds leads ultimately to the final outcome of self-destruction.

Sad to say, this description is not merely a theological description, for it has frequently been illustrated in history. And unless by some means the course of sin is checked in a human life, it tends to run in the same direction. Men lack the ability to view themselves objectively because their minds get tainted to a point where it is hard to face un-pleasant facts about themselves. This is why they need the Bible to serve as their guide and example.

2. The Psychological Effects of Sin

Dr. Lewis J. Sherrill has interpreted the experience of sin with the terms of guilt, anxiety, and hostility. (Guilt and Redemption, John Knox Press, Richmond, Va.) Our sense of guilt leads us to run away from God, as Adam and Eve did in the garden. We may do this with excuses which become reasons for neglecting the appointed means of spiritual growth. The guilt may become deeply rooted in personality so that anxiety develops over the fact that we hate to face our sin as it is. Therefore we try to keep it from coming to the surface of our minds and transfer that anxiety to the many other things that our minds conjure up as possibilities. Financial status, physical health, social prestige, or something else becomes a matter of great concern. Because of this strain of anxiety upon personality, we become hostile to ourselves but transfer that hostility often to other people. This hostility may be toward our own selves in a way that produces stomach ulcers or heart trouble. It may be toward a parent, a husband, a wife, a child, a minister, a church, a friend. It may be toward God in Christ. It will find a dozen reasons for not doing the one thing that is needful in starting a new life. But the quality of the reasons is not nearly so important as the fact that they prevent the person from finding his peace and joy in Jesus Christ.

3. Rationalization As An Escape From the Reality of Sin

Two particular forms of false reasoning (sometimes called rationalization) are sufficiently prevalent to deserve mention.

A. Attributing the Best Motives to Ourselves

Let us imagine that two men who are business competitors happen to be officers in the same church. And let us suppose that in the mind of the one who has been less successful than the other there is a jealousy or hostility deep down within his soul. Some decision has to be made about a change in the church program. One man favors it and the other opposes it. The one opposing, who already has a grudge he cannot bring into the open, finds a matter of principle involved. He can stick with that matter of principle without exposing his grudge of which he is not proud. In that way he may get the better of his business competitor, and at the same time attribute to himself the best possible motive for his action.

Of course this kind of practice is not limited to business competitors. It finds expression among children, youth, and grownups alike. But it is a common weakness that must be guarded against at all times.

Another common way that sin destroys human personality is by enabling individuals to find good reasons for unworthy acts. A young service man was talking with a minister about his wife. He was going home to get possession of his child because he could not trust his wife. He heard that she was having dates with other men. When he was asked how he proposed to care for the child, it developed that he had a girl friend near the base who would take care of it for him. By some twist of reasoning he had convinced himself that while his wife should be faithful to him or lose custody of her child, he could be unfaithful and claim custody through her failure. He was seeking a good reason for his unworthy conduct.

Such a man is following the logic of Plutarch in his advice to wives not to be angry with their husbands when they indulged in some intrigue with a maid or harlot. "The wife should realize," he said, "that the husband is indulging his passions with another woman out of respect for his wife." This seems a very peculiar way to show respect for one's wife, but it reveals how an intelligent man can find good reasons for unworthy acts. It also reveals the destructive power of sin in the human mind. This destructive power of sin which works so subtly must never be ignored or underestimated, for it is a constant peril to one's moral and spiritual life.

C. CONSIDERATION OF THE PUNISHMENT WHICH IS DUE FOR SIN

The above discussion indicates that sin brings its own punishment. Someone may ask, "Is not God arbitrary in punishing people for sin?" The answer is a decided NO. The punishment is not arbitrarily given from without human personality, but developed naturally from within. This is true because of the evil character of sin and because of the constant working of sin in the human mind and heart.

C. S. Lewis' "Screwtape Letters" show clearly how evil forces are constantly at work to prevent a man from becoming his best self. At every turn in the road the wormwoods of Satan are at work. When these forces find a willing ear on the part of human beings, they continue their destructive activity. And man's nature is such that it seems easier to follow the easy road to destruction and lack of purpose and self-satisfaction than it is to follow the high road to redemption. To surrender the best self in each real battle is to put habit on the side of failure. And sin builds up the power of habit, giving good reasons for bad choices until they seem to be justified. This becomes easier still when the current of public opinion flows in its favor.

1. What Men Deserve

What ought God to do with men who are so bent on ther own moral and spiritual destruction? They have no moral claim on Him whom they forsake in thought, word, and deed. But thanks be to God, He offers His pardon and power to all who believe. He does not leave Himself without witness as the Holy Spirit works in men to bring God's own to salvation. God will not condone sin, but He will forgive it. He will not destroy man's moral nature but He will transform it. And even though sin is not completely overcome in this life, the final and ultimate victory will be the Lord's. How this is possible will be shown in the next few studies.

2. What Men Ought to Do

What ought men to do about their sin? First, let them recognize it. They will never get rid of sin by denying its existence. Second, let them heed God's call to forsake it. "Let the wicked forsake his way, and the unrighteous man his thoughts; let him return to the Lord, that he may have mercy on him, and to our God, for he will abundantly pardon." (Isaiah 55:7.) Third, let them seek God's cleansing power in Jesus Christ. "If we confess our sins, he is faithful and just, and will forgive our sins and cleanse us from all unrighteousness." (I John 1:9.)

WORKSHEET

1. We need to recognize our_____as it is in order to achieve

   _____.

2. Four possible kinds of moral worlds suggested are:

   a.

   b.

   c.

   d.

3. Moral choices are important for us because_____

   _____.

4. According to the Presbyterian Standards,_____and_____
   not only brought punishment on themselves, but transmitted their
   guilt to all coming generations.

5. Three replies suggested to persons who object to this idea are:

   a.

   b.

   c.

6. Three steps in the downward path of man described in Romans 1:18-32 are:

   a.

   b.

   c.

7. Dr. Sherrill has interpreted the consequences of sin in terms of guilt, _____and_____.

8. In order to get rid of their sin, men should:

   a.

   b.

   c.

CHAPTER VI

Our Means of Salvation

INTRODUCTION

A college student had participated in a discussion about man's sin and came a few days later to the leader to say:

"Your description of what Presbyterians believe about human sinfulness left me somewhat depressed and uncomfortable. I did not feel exactly like a worm, but I did not feel very good either."

To such a person we may reply: (1) It is much better to be realistic about human nature than it is to look at ourselves through rose-colored glasses. The more honestly we face the awful facts about ourselves, the better we will be able to deal with them. (2) This somewhat pessimistic view of man as a sinner is not final and is not the the total view of Presbyterians about what man may become. It is the starting point in dealing with man, but it is not the goal toward which Presbyterians move in either thought or experience. Let us never mistake the starting point for the goal. (3) Such a view of man as we have considered leaves us dissatisfied and therefore encourages us to lay hold on the means of salvation which God has provided. Let us therefore turn our thoughts to the first means of salvation, which is the election of believers by God.

A. THE MEANING OF ELECTION

The doctrine of election is defined in our Confession in terms of the decrees of God, which we studied in a previous chapter, and in terms of the covenant of works which Adam and Eve failed to keep. Therefore God in His mercy initiated the covenant of grace, which is described in these words:

"Man, by his fall, having made himself incapable of life by that covenant, the Lord was pleased to make a second, commonly called the covenant of grace: wherein he freely offered unto sinners life and salvation by Jesus Christ, requiring of them faith in him, that they may be saved, and promising to give unto all those that are ordained unto life, his Holy Spirit, to make them willing and able to believe." (Chapter VII, Article III)

This covenant was a covenant of promise in the Old Testament dispensation. Through circumcision, the sacrifices, the prophecies, and other means the promises of God to provide salvation in Christ were made increasingly clear. In the New Testament dispensation, this covenant is a covenant of fulfillment in Jesus Christ. He is the Mediator who is revealed in the preaching and teaching of the word, and in the faithful administration of the sacraments of Baptism and the Lord's Supper. This covenant is not two covenants, but one. It is claimed by all of the spiritual seed of Abraham through their faith in Christ. It is called a covenant of grace.

1. CHARACTERISTICS OF THE COVENANT OF GRACE

Three characteristics of this covenant of grace should be mentioned. The first is that God freely offers life and salvation through Jesus Christ to all sinners. The Gospel is offered to all men. It is not withheld by God from those who may not be among the elect.

The second characteristic is that God requires of sinners a saving faith in Jesus Christ as Lord and Saviour. God offers this salvation in the Gospel, but it is not given until it is received. Let us illustrate this important principle. If a parent should offer his child a nickel, it remains an offer until the child reaches up his hand and takes it. Then it becomes a gift. So also God offers salvation in Jesus Christ. That offer becomes a gift when a repentant sinner claims it in faith. The meaning of a saving faith will be discussed in the next chapter. It is mentioned here because it is ordained as God's way of providing salvation to believers.

The third characteristic is that God promises to give the Holy Spirit to all who are ordained to eternal life, to make them willing and able to believe. In the previous chapter we considered the fact that sin prevents persons from thinking clearly or from acting nobly. Even to a historian not posing as a theologian, the human race seems to be bent on its own destruction. But God by His Spirit reaches out and lays hold on many human hearts to pull them back from their self-destruction. It is as though men were walking in darkness toward a precipice and some hear within them a voice of warning to turn back to the bridge which spans the precipice. God gives His Holy Spirit to make them willing and able to believe. Concerning the work of the Holy Spirit in leading the elect to salvation, the Confession says:

"The dispensation of the gospel is especially committed to him. He prepares the way for it, accompanies it with his persuasive power, and urges its message upon the reason and conscience of men, so that they who reject its merciful offer are not only without excuse, but are also guilty of resisting the Holy Spirit." (Chapter IX, Article II)

2. THE DOCTRINE OF ELECTION DOES NOT EXCLUDE BELIEVERS

Someone may ask, does not this doctrine of election work arbitrarily to exclude some who otherwise might believe? No, it does not. Jesus promised to receive all who came unto Him. Presbyterians believe that He will keep to His promise. At the same time, they believe that God has the final word on every one of His creatures. Jesus commanded His disciples to preach the Gospel to every creature. The Gospel says that there is no other means of salvation than that which comes by faith in Jesus Christ. No person who has heard the Gospel may blame God for his failure to respond, for as God offers His grace, man must take it and use it. Those who felt that they were among the elect did so, not by reading the eternal mind of God, but by claiming for themselves the grace of God in Christ. They acted freely, and they felt responsible for their choice. It is because our knowledge of the infinite ways of God is so limited that we are urged to handle the high mystery of predestination with special prudence and care (Confession of Faith, Chapter III, Article VIII.) We must recognize the fact that God takes the initiative and offers the Holy Spirit. We must also remember that it is only when we take this offer and exercise a saving faith that redemption becomes effective in us.

3. Key Points Summarizing the Doctrine of Election

Some key points which summarize the doctrine of election may be mentioned. The *first* is that God is sovereign. At the same time He is holy and righteous, loving and merciful. The *second* is that man is free to choose within the limits of the moral universe which is created by God. His choice is actual and uncoerced within the realm where he has learned to live. The *third* is that election in the Bible is always for a purpose. Abraham, Moses, and the prophets were called for a purpose. The Hebrew nation existed to witness to God in a pagan world. The apostles were called according to a purpose. They were sent forth to witness to the Gospel of Jesus Christ. Believers in the church were also among those "called according to His purpose." They also were called to witness to their faith. God's purpose for believers today is the same. We are not to attempt to satisfy our intellectual curiosity as to who is elect and who is not, which is the prerogative of God. We are rather to accept God's election for the purpose of making us into His likeness and to make us good witnesses of His transforming power.

Fourth, as a consequence of his attitudes and habits in life, man is headed for his own destruction. If left to himself, man will destroy himself. *Fifth,* God's purpose to save some from everlasting punishment through their faith in Christ is according to His love and mercy, not according to man's deserving. Let every believer therefore be grateful, not proud. For he is an object of God's grace, not a person who lifted himself by his own bootstraps.

Since we do not and cannot ever know on earth who are the elect of God except through their faith in Christ, let us not be led into

[64]

fruitless speculation. Let us realize our calling as Christians, and let us be faithful in the task of preaching the glorious Gospel of Christ to every creature. Then we can have the drive of the doctrine of election without the harmful speculation which turns it from a glorious doctrine into an academic debate.

B. THE MEANING OF EFFECTUAL CALLING

Effectual calling means that God always does His part in man's salvation. The best short definition of effectual calling is given in the Shorter Catechism, Answer to Question 31:

> "Effectual calling is the work of God's Spirit, whereby, convincing us of our sin and misery, enlightening our minds in the knowledge of Christ, and renewing our wills, he doth persuade and enable us to embrace Jesus Christ freely offered to us in the Gospel."

1. FIVE FEATURES OF EFFECTUAL CALLING

Let us underscore five distinct features of effectual calling as these are suggested by this definition and described more fully in our Confession of Faith, Chapter XII.

First, effectual calling is the work of God's Spirit. The starting point is God's Spirit, not man's decision. For man is not capable of making the right decision without the help of the Holy Spirit.

Second, the Holy Spirit convinces us of our sin and misery. We may suppose that we are doing all right because we compare ourselves with other sinners who are very much like we are. Imagine a group of men walking in the darkness with only a small candle to guide them. Suppose they were asked whether they needed more light than they were accustomed to using. They might well refuse unless and until a searchlight was put at their disposal and their eyes became accustomed to its light. Then they would wonder why they had ever walked in the semidarkness for so long. The apostle Paul had to be convinced that the road he traveled as a persecutor was wrong before he was willing to walk in the light of the Gospel. He had to be convinced of his sin and misery before he was willing to seek a better way of living. The Holy Spirit convinces us that our old life is bad and that we need something better.

Third, the Holy Spirit enlightens our minds in the knowledge of Christ. The summary of what we believe about Christ in the Apostles' Creed points to what the Holy Spirit teaches us about Jesus Christ. He is God's Son, incarnate in the flesh, crucified for our sins, raised for our justification, and now interceding for us at the right hand of God the Father, coming again in His good time to judge the world, Lord of believers throughout eternity. We do not come to the recognition of the redemptive meaning of Jesus Christ by ourselves. The Holy Spirit enlightens our minds to enable us to see Him as Lord and Saviour, and to know that He is *our* Saviour. He redeems each one of us who believe. His love constrains us and moves us to commit ourselves to Him.

Fourth, the Holy Spirit renews our wills. The words of Paul, "What shall I do, Lord?" (Acts 22:10), mark a new centering of Paul's will. He had been doing what he willed, assuming that God approved because the Jewish leaders in Jerusalem approved. Now he was in the process of ceasing to do his own will, and of seeking the will of Christ. This change of will is the work of the Holy Spirit in effectual calling. It results in being willing to do God's will rather than our own.

Fifth, the Holy Spirit persuades and enables us to embrace Jesus Christ as Saviour and Lord as He is offered to us freely in the Gospel. This is not coercion, but persuasion. It is not leaving us to act of our own power, but bringing us to act by His power. This effectual calling leads us to commit ourselves willingly to Christ to be used by Him in whatever way He sees fit. From recognizing that He gave His life for us it leads us to give our lives to Him. This is the response of the believer to the Holy Spirit. This is the acceptance of God's calling as effectual for you and for me.

2. The Calling of Elect Infants

It is natural for someone to ask what happens to infants who do not have opportunity to reach an age of decision and hence to claim their effectual calling. The Confession of Faith answers the question in this manner:

"Elect infants, dying in infancy, are regenerated and saved by Christ through the Spirit, who worketh when, and where, and how he pleaseth. So also are all other elect persons who are incapable of being outwardly called by the ministry of the word." (Chapter XII, Article III)

While therefore Presbyterians hold to the doctrine that faith in Christ is the only means of salvation, they also affirm that God will provide in fairness and in love for all who have not the opportunity to receive and to embrace the outward preaching of Jesus Christ as Saviour. It is ours to teach and to preach the Gospel to everyone. It is God's to save all whom He chooses to save by this means or any other dictated by His holy will.

C. THE MEANING OF JUSTIFICATION

Justification is defined in the Shorter Catechism as follows:
"Justification is an act of God's free grace, wherein He pardoneth

all our sins, and accepteth us in as righteous in his sight, only for the righteousness of Christ, imputed to us, and received by faith alone." (Answer to Question 33.)

Let us observe four things about this definition of justification. First, it is an act of God's free grace. As an act of God's free grace it is not based on His foreknowledge of man's goodness. It is rooted in the purpose and the will of God from all eternity.

Second, justification wipes out past sin. It is as though every person were carrying a burden on his back and suddenly, like Christian in *Pilgrim's Progress*, had the burden loosed from his back. It is like the experience of the woman whom Jesus forgave in the temple when her accusers refused to cast the first stone at her. He said, "Neither do I condemn you; go, and do not sin again." He told her the past was forgiven and that she could now lead a new life.

Third, in justification, believers are accepted as righteous for Christ's sake. They are not accepted because they are doing better works than anyone else. They are not accepted because they are worthy. They are declared to be righteous before God because of the perfect obedience of Jesus Christ. His righteousness acts like a cloak to cover the sins of believers. God sees believers as those whose sins are covered through the sacrificial love of Christ their Saviour and Lord.

Fourth, justification is received by faith alone. Presbyterians do not attempt to achieve justification through their works. They do work to become what they are declared to be in Christ. They put their faith to work to demonstrate its genuineness and to express their gratitude to God for providing their redemption in Christ. They open the windows of their soul, as it were, to receive the Spirit who cleanses them and who enables them to strive for the obedience of the sons of God.

D. THE MEANING OF ADOPTION

Adoption is defined in the Shorter Catechism, Answer 34, as follows: "Adoption is an act of God's free grace, whereby we are received into the number, and have a right to all the privileges, of the sons of God."

Like election, effectual calling, and justification, adoption is an act of God's free grace. It is His purpose in operation, not man's achievement of merit. Adoption by God is something like adoption by human parents. Parents adopt children, and these children in turn accept their adoption as children.

Two important results follow adoption. The first is a sense of belonging to God's family. Believers are no longer orphans before God, but adopted children. They share in the sufferings, the joys and the blessings of family life. They become a part of the church, which is a fellowship of persons becoming saints on the earth. The second result is that believers enjoy all the privileges of sonship. They have the family name and a share in their inheritance with Christ. God's bank account belongs to them. His promises are theirs to have and to hold. If therefore their recognition of sin makes Presbyterians feel like worms, their acceptance of their adoption as sons of God brings them into a feeling of belonging to the most glorious fellowship in heaven or on earth.

E. THE MEANING OF SANCTIFICATION

"Sanctification is the work of God's free grace, whereby we are renewed in the whole man after the image of God, and are enabled more and more to die unto sin, and to live unto righteousness." (Answer to Question 35 in the Shorter Catechism.)

Let us recognize the four characteristics of sanctification mentioned in this definition.

First, sanctification is a work of God's free grace. It is not described merely as an act, but as something which is in process for some time. One may be declared righteous before God by an act of adoption. But one becomes the kind of son that one is declared to be by a process of spiritual growth. We work out our salvation only as God is constantly at work within us to will and to accomplish His good pleasure. Thus sanctification is a work of God's free grace within us.

Second, by sanctification we are transformed and renewed within the whole man. It is something like grafting the bud of an apple tree on the stock of a walnut tree. The apple tree is produced and the stock becomes a part of the apple tree.

Sanctification results from regeneration. No woman would place a geranium pot in a rose garden and expect the geranium to bloom like a rose. Why? Because the life of the rose is not in the geranium plant. If a woman wishes another plant to bloom like the rose, she will get a cutting from the parent rose properly rooted. Then she will water, fertilize, and cultivate this new plant until it blooms like the rose. It will bloom like the rose because it has the life of the parent rosebush in it.

When the Christian is born again through the reception of the life of Christ through the Holy Spirit, he has a little of the life of Christ in him. This new life, when properly cultivated by the appointed means of spiritual growth, keeps on spreading until it roots out the old life and supplants it with the new. The inner man is renewed and transformed by the power of the Spirit of God at work within him. This is why and how he becomes a new creature in Christ. This renewal may be more sudden in some than in others. It is a process by which believers are remade into the moral and spiritual image of God in Christ.

Third, by sanctification the Holy Spirit enables us more and more to die unto sin. It will be recalled that sin is a transgression of the revealed will of God. It is also a failure to measure up to the full will of God. By sanctification we die more and more to the pride and rebellion which is expressed in disobedience to God's will. More and more we die to the laziness and self-satisfaction which leaves us willing to live half-heartedly for Christ.

Fourth, in sanctification the Holy Spirit enables us to live more and more unto righteousness. As the Spirit of God works in us, we come to accept new and high goals in life. We have wonderful things to live for. We seek to glorify God and enjoy Him forever. We keep straining forward to the things which are before us as followers of Christ. We live in the dawn of a great surprise day by day. New life is ours as we enter into a new obedience to the whole will of God. Increasingly and constantly we grow into the likeness of Christ.

While therefore it is true that Presbyterians face their sin realistically, they do not believe that this is their end or goal. They believe in a new life in Christ. Through election, effectual calling, justification, adoption and sanctification they are transformed into the spiritual image of Christ who dwells in them by His Holy Spirit. This is the new life to which Christians are called. It is the new life toward which, by God's grace, they strive day by day.

WORKSHEET

1. The purpose of recognizing our sinfulness is to encourage us to

_____.

2. The covenant of grace is a covenant of_____in the Old Testament dispensation, and a covenant of_____ in the New.

3. Three characteristics of this covenant of grace are:

   a.

   b.

   c.

4. The election of God is not unfair and arbitrary, for it does not deny to man the right to _____ within the limits set by God.

5. The doctrine of election is not designed to stimulate endless speculation but purposive_____ by Christian people.

6. Five things I have learned about effectual calling are:_____

_____

_____

_____

7. Four factors in justification are:
    a.
    b.
    c.
    d.

8. Two results that follow adoption are:
    a.
    b.

9. Four characteristics of sanctification are:_____

_____

_____

_____

CHAPTER VII

Our Experience of Salvation

INTRODUCTION

A group of young people were having a "bull session." One of them who was not a Presbyterian, asked a Presbyterian friend, "You don't believe in that stuff which says, 'Once saved, always saved,' do you?"

The Presbyterian friend answered affirmatively from a sense of loyalty, but not from a real understanding of the meaning of salvation. For this reason, at his first opportunity he sought the help of his minister to get some light on this subject. We will include in this chapter some of the things he learned. The most important thing he learned was that salvation is an experience, not primarily a dogma. It is something that happens to a believer, not just a doctrine that Presbyterians are expected to defend. It grows out of the purpose of God to save and the gift of His Spirit which is received in effectual calling.

Salvation may be described as something provided once for all by Jesus Christ. It is also an experience which is constantly in process, including the elements discussed in the last chapter. It is an experience which reaches a climax in some moment or moments of worship and decision, and which has existing results in the life of the believer. It is an experience of being transformed from within so that Christ may live fully in the believer.

A. THE PLACE OF CHRIST IN OUR EXPERIENCE

For the Christian, salvation centers in Jesus Christ and in a personal relationship with Him. Jesus Christ is accepted as He is presented in the Gospel—as the Son of God who became incarnate in the flesh through the Virgin birth, and as the crucified and risen Lord who provides redemption for believers. The way in which He united the qualities of deity and humanity are never fully explained any more than the Trinity is explained. The fact that He did is the clear indication of the scriptures and the faith of the church through the centuries.

Christ is presented in the Westminster Standards as prophet, priest, and king. He is the prophet who declares the whole will of God concerning man's salvation. He is the priest who became the perfect sacrifice for the sins of believers in all ages. He is the king who rules over the universe, and who gives the final victory to His own.

The Christ who is described in Philippians 2:5-11 and in other parts of the New Testament is the Lord and Saviour of believers. The relationship between the crucified, risen, living Lord and the believer is a

[71]

very personal relationship. It leads the believer to know in experience the meaning of the words of Paul: "It is no longer I who lives, but Christ who lives in me." (Galatians 2:20) In this kind of relationship with Christ, it is expected that a Presbyterian will want to be united with the body of Christ, which is his church. The union with the church is a means of achieving full salvation in Christ, who is its head.

B. THE MEANING OF REPENTANCE UNTO LIFE

While the various parts of the experience of repentance cannot be divorced from one another, they may be described logically in separate ways. Effectual calling is the activity of God. Repentance unto life is the response of believing man. This repentance has in it at least four essential elements.

1. It Begins With the Holy Spirit and the Word

First, repentance unto life begins with the Holy Spirit and the word of God. We cannot explain exactly how it is true, but we know that it is true that when the scriptures are read or expounded, the Holy Spirit acts in a special way to convince and convert sinners so that they may turn to God and commit their lives to Him. Repentance does not begin in a vacuum, but in an experience of the truth of God's revealed will which is made effective through the activity of the Holy Spirit.

2. It Roots in a Realization of the Heinousness of Sin

Second, repentance unto life roots in a realization of the heinousness of sin. No matter how good a moral life we might have lived, and no matter how good we have considered ourselves in comparison with our neighbors, repentance unto life leads us to compare our righteousness with the righteousness of Christ, and to stand condemned because we are sinful in His sight. Just as it is possible to ignore the soot in snow cream until one gets it under a light, so it is possible to ignore our sinfulness until we see it in the light of Christ. Then we recognize a sinfulness which we as individuals confess directly to God. This includes both general sinfulness and particular sins of which we are aware. It bespeaks a confidence that God will hear and forgive us when we come in genuine repentance. No works of penance are required in the scriptures, and no works of penance are sufficient to give us merit before God.

3. It Claims Christ's Mercy for us as Sinners

While all of the parts of repentance unto life accompany each other, a third logical part is the realization of the mercy and love of God in Jesus Christ. The story of the love of God in Jesus Christ is no longer the Gospel for believers in general, but the Gospel for each one of us.

By it we know that Christ died for you and for me. This truth was presented symbolically in *Pilgrim's Progress* when Christian stood before Christ on the cross and realized that Christ died for him. The burden which he carried on his back slipped off, never to return. He was free from his sin through the redemptive love and mercy of Jesus Christ. He dared to take the forgiveness which was provided for him, and to start forth again on his journey to the celestial city of light.

4. IT ISSUES IN A NEW TURNING TO GOD FOR OBEDIENCE

The fourth phase of the experience of repentance unto life is a new turning to God for obedience. We believe that the only way to root out old habits is to form new ones. This is well illustrated by the experience of Paul on the way to Damascus. He thought he was doing the will of God when he persecuted the Christians. However, he became convicted by the Holy Spirit, turned from his sinfulness, committed himself to Christ as Saviour and Lord, and went into Damascus to a new life of obedience. He did not at first know what was to follow, but he learned step by step through the new spirit of obedience. Conviction by the Holy Spirit, a realization of his sinfulness, an understanding that Jesus Christ was his personal Saviour, and an endeavor after a new obedience to the will of God thus became a part of Paul's experience of repentance unto life. So also it is with all who come into a saving faith.

C. THE MEANING OF A SAVING FAITH

A member of the church asks, "What do you mean by a saving faith? I have been hearing that expression all my life, but I am not sure I know what it means."

Let us attempt a reply. A saving faith begins with the provision of God in Christ for our salvation. God by His Spirit calls and moves the elect to believe. God takes the initiative. But a saving faith is generated in man when he becomes receptive to the moving of God's Spirit to enter into an experience of repentance unto life.

1. IT IS THE COMMITMENT OF THE WHOLE LIFE TO CHRIST

One who has watched small boys learning to swim has doubtless been impressed with the way they fight to keep from letting themselves go in the water. But a wise lifeguard teaches them to let themselves go. He teaches them to float. They learn to float by taking a deep breath and letting themselves go in the water. They discover that as they relax and let themselves go, the water holds them up. They still have to learn to pull with their arms, to kick with their feet, and to breathe properly before they can swim.

Exercising a saving faith is like learning to swim. It is letting oneself go and letting God take control of his life. It is the response which makes possible the new birth and the new growth as a child of God. Faith is that response to the moving of God's Spirit which leads to the union of the Spirit and human personality. As a constant attitude of mind and heart it says to God, in the words of Frances R. Havergal's great hymn:

"Take my life and let it be,
Consecrated, Lord to thee;
Take my moments and my days,
Let them flow in ceaseless praise."

Whether it be time, or hands or feet, whether it be will or heart, whether it be love or self, the Christian at his best commits all that he is or has to Christ. But he receives it back again to be used as a sacred trust in faith, dedicated to the accomplishment of the will of God.

2. IT IS A CONTINUOUS HABIT AND PRACTICE OF LIFE

A saving faith is not something that begins and ceases after a period of decision. It is an attitude which continues throughout this life and throughout eternity. It gives a sense of mission in every vocation. In business, in home-making, in studying, in Home or World Mission service it makes all that one does for Christ significant and meaningful. It dissolves fears and gives victory over a feeling of frustration. It keeps the believer united with Christ as the branch is united with the vine. It enables the believer to take the power and life of the vine and to produce the fruit of the Spirit of God. This is what we mean by a saving faith. It is a living faith, a transforming faith, a triumphant faith. It can never be defeated, for it claims the victory of Christ in the daily experiences of life.

D. THE JOY OF PERSEVERANCE BY HIS GRACE

Like the doctrine of predestination, the doctrine of perseverance should not be considered in isolation. Presbyterians believe in the saving and keeping power of God, but they believe in the genuine faith which must be exercised by those who are kept by the power of God. They believe in the perseverance of the saints for the saints who persevere. This is well stated in the Larger Catechism, Question 79, as follows:

Q. May not true believers, by reason of their imperfections, and the many temptations and sins they are overtaken with, fall away from the state of grace?

A. True believers, by reason of the unchangeable love of God, and his decree and covenant to give them perseverance, their inseparable union with Christ, his continual intercession for them, and the Spirit and the seed of God abiding in them, can neither totally nor finally fall away from the state of grace, but are kept by the power of God through faith unto salvation."

1. The Experience of True Believers

Because this doctrine has so frequently been misunderstood, let us study it carefully. Observe that the question does not point to every person whose name may be on a church roll. It deals with true believers, persons who have entered into a genuine and transforming experience with Jesus Christ. It does not refer to everyone who says, "Lord, Lord," but with those who express their faith in obedience day by day. They are like those who do the things Jesus teaches and hence build on the rock of faith put to work. They are not like the hearers who fail to obey, and hence build a house on the sand. (See Matthew 7:24-27 or Luke 6:46-49). The doctrine of the perseverance of the saints requires that the saints persevere.

2. The Keeping Power of God's Love

What further reasons may be given for believing in the keeping power of God? These are given in the answer to the Catechism question which has been quoted above. First, believers who are genuine believers rest in the unchangeable love of God. This redemptive love becomes a tremendous power for good in their lives. Just as the love of a saintly mother or father or wife or husband holds many a person back from evil conduct, so the unchanging love of God, in even greater measure, holds genuine believers in the path of light and life.

This redemptive love is expressed in God's decree and covenant to give true believers power to persevere. He is able and willing to keep His own. He kept Abraham through many trials and failures. He kept the prophets through much heartbreak and rejection. He kept Paul through a stormy and trying ministry. He kept John even in his banishment to Patmos in his old age. He has kept the saints who dared to trust Him through the ages. God's purpose stands firm. He is able to keep all that we commit unto Him. Thus the question is not so much whether we can hold on to God as it is whether we are willing to be held by Him. This latter willingnes is at the root of His saving and keeping power even when we are weak and sinful.

3. The Inseparable Union With Christ

A further reason for confidence in perseverance is the believer's inseparable union with Christ. Some of His life is in the believer. The

[75]

two walk together down the road of life. The living Christ by His Spirit leads the believer day by day. This new life does not begin after physical death, but is a present experience. As John 5:24 says, "Truly, truly, I say unto you, he who hears my word and believes him who sent me, has eternal life; he does not come into judgment, but has passed from death to life." The word for *life* is a word which denotes the life of God made available to men through Jesus Christ. Thus Christ and the believer are more inseparably bound than are a group of mountain climbers who have a rope tied around their waists. His footing does not slip even though ours momentarily may do so. Because we are bound with Him, we have confidence in His power to keep us.

4. THE CONTINUAL INTERCESSION OF CHRIST

Furthermore, we know that we will be kept by the power of God because we believe that Christ's intercession will avail for us as it availed for Peter. Jesus knew that Satan was trying to destroy Peter's faith during the dark days when He was being tried and crucified. He warned Peter that he would deny his Lord. But He also said, "But I have prayed for you that your faith may not fail; and when you have turned again, strengthen your brethren." (Luke 22:32). This knowledge that Jesus was interceding for him, and the confidence that Peter would come back to be a rock of strength to his brethren lies behind the great power demonstrated by Peter in the book of Acts. Since Jesus' intercession availed for Peter who failed temporarily, it will also avail for others who genuinely believe in Christ as Lord and Saviour.

5. THE INDWELLING SEED OF CHRIST

Another reason why true believers have confidence in the keeping power of God is the fact that the seed of God is in them. We have already suggested that the Spirit of God unites with the heart of the believer to reproduce the life of Christ in him. We call this experience regeneration or new birth. By whatever name it is called, the experience is one which gives an inner confidence. Some Christians have been puzzled over the statement in I John 3:6 that the person who has the seed of God in him cannot sin. If we were careful to observe the tense of the verb used, we would know it means that the person who has the seed of God in him cannot make sin the daily habit and practice of his life. This is true and is not in conflict with the teaching in I John 1:8-2:2 that no one can say he has never committed acts of sin. All who commit acts of sin must seek forgiveness through Jesus Christ. Even though they do commit acts of sin for which they must be forgiven, they have the life of God in them which enables them more and more to die unto sin and to live unto righteousness.

For these reasons it is stated that true believers cannot totally nor finally fall away from the state of grace, but are kept by the power of God *through faith* unto salvation. The over-simplified dictum, "Once saved, always saved," has the practical effect of nullifying the conditions set by God Himself, and of ignoring the relationships and reasons why Presbyterians believe in the perseverance of the saints. Such loose and one-sided over-simplification has probably done more harm than good to persons who have not taken the trouble to understand the basis on which this great doctrine rests. It is no credit either to faith or to God to state a position which invites misunderstanding and argument and rejection of the rich experience of knowing the keeping power of God through our faith in Jesus Christ.

E. THE ASSURANCE OF SALVATION

The grounds of Christian assurance have already been suggested in the preceding discussion. Let us suggest a few more.

1. The Importance of Christian Experience

If one should ask, "How can I be sure that the keeping power of God is mine?", we would point once again to the doctrine presented above. But we would do more. We would emphasize the importance of developing assurance by experience. Suppose a boy stands on the bank of a pool and repeats over and over again, "I am sure I can swim," but never ventures into the water. What will happen to his assurance? But if instead of constantly repeating his assertion, he gets into the water and learns to swim, he will develop confidence so that he does not have to keep on repeating something to himself.

This is a parable of the Christian life. Many Christians want assurance based only on logical arguments. They do not want to develop assurance through faithful obedience. They are not genuine believers, but persons who say, "Lord, Lord." To be sure, they may have to take another Christian's word for Christ's keeping power at first. They do the same thing when they ride a new bus to town. But after several rides they know for themselves. And after several experiences in which the believer has acted in faith, he gains confidence in God's power to save and keep him. The more he acts in faith, the more assured he becomes. For twenty centuries believers have tested the truth of the Gospel. Those who have lived by the Christian faith have found the promises of God trustworthy. Therefore they feel assured that God will fulfill all of His promises, including those concerning salvation and the life to come.

2. The Indwelling Presence of the Holy Spirit

Assurance comes to us also through the indwelling presence of the Holy Spirit. Although temptations may come, and trials may temporarily shake our faith, though disappointment, sorrow and bereavement may be experienced, the indwelling Spirit of God enables us to know that God's way is best in the long run. His grace is sufficient for our every need. This experience is something like a cork on the water. A strong pull may temporarily submerge it, but it exerts a constant pressure to rise until it floats again on the water. It is something like the experience presented in *Pilgrim's Progress*, where the devil was pouring water to put out the fires of faith in one room, but on the other side of the wall the Spirit of God was pouring on oil to keep the fires of faith aflame. The indwelling Spirit enables us to know that as God raised up Jesus and turned His death into a glorious redemptive victory for the church, so God will turn our faithful service into an experience of ultimate victory. Thus we gain assurance in our faith and through our faith.

3. The Habit of Obedience

Our assurance of salvation also grows through our obedience. The faith of the centurion, who spoke out of a soldier's concept of obedience to authority, caused Jesus to marvel. (See Luke 7:1-10.) It is true that Paul was assured on the way to Damascus that he heard the voice of the risen Christ. But after thirty years of service to Christ, in which he had suffered ridicule, imprisonment, beatings, shipwrecks, and many attempts to take his life, Paul could write to Timothy, in words which might be translated literally, "I know whom I have believed, and am fully convinced that he is able to guard all that I have committed unto Him against that day." Paul was much more sure then than he was when he began his life of obedience to the will of his living Lord.

If there be some who doubt the possibility of assurance, let them develop assurance in their own Christian experience. But let them know that assurance comes through trust in the promises of God, through the indwelling presence of the Holy Spirit, and through obedience to the will of God in daily living.

SUMMARY

In this chapter we have presented certain basic beliefs of Presbyterianism. We have suggested that salvation is an experience which centers in Jesus Christ and a personal relationship with Him. Repentance unto life is the corollary to effectual calling in that it represents man's response to the call of God from the old life to the new. A saving faith is a vital and active faith generated by God's Spirit which leads the believer into a living union with Christ, as a branch is united with the vine. Perseverance is possible only through the enabling grace of God, but requires on man's part a life of obedience and stedfastness. Believers not only are kept by the power of God, but may also experience assurance of their salvation if they are willing to live a life of faith and obedience. These doctrines give comfort and assurance to Presbyterians, and strengthen them in their faith. They undergird the kind of living which demonstrates the transforming power of God in the daily routine of life.

WORKSHEET

1. Salvation is_____once for all by Jesus Christ.

2. Salvation is_____by believers as a constant process.

3. Salvation centers in _____ _____ and not in regulations or dogmas advanced by a particular branch of the Christian church.

4. Repentance unto life consists of the following:

   a.

   b.

   c.

   d.

5. Exercising a saving faith in Christ is like learning to swim. It requires a complete_____of the whole self to Christ, and a consistent obedience to His will for our lives.

6. The popular statement, "Once saved, always saved" is hardly an adequate presentation of the doctrine of_____.

7. The doctrine of the perseverance of the saints requires that the saints_____.

8. Presbyterians who are genuine believers in Christ know that they are kept by His power because:

   a.

   b.

   c.

   d.

9. Assurance that we are saved comes through:

   a.

   b.

   c.

CHAPTER VIII

Our Fellowship in the Church

INTRODUCTION

Those who have followed this study thus far have doubtless reached the conclusion that salvation is an individual experience. It is an individual experience, but historically this individual experience has developed in the fellowship of the church. Ordinarily the individual experience is deeper, richer, and more meaningful because it arises and is developed in the fellowship of the church.

Presbyterians believe in the church. They hold a high doctrine of the church. They follow John Calvin in recognizing both an invisible and a visible church. Let us begin with these topics as we consider some of the important things that Presbyterians believe about the church.

A. THE INVISIBLE CHURCH

The Confession of Faith, Chapter XXVII, Article I, defines the invisible church in these words:

> "The catholic or universal church, which is invisible, consists of the whole number of the elect, that have been, are, or shall be gathered into one, under Christ the head thereof; and is the spouse, the body, the fullness of Him that filleth all in all."

Observe that the church consists of God's elect in all ages. This church is described as universal or catholic. This does not mean, of course, the Roman Catholic church which recognizes only the authority of the Roman hierarchy and the pope in Rome. It means all believers in all ages, including those who are or have been associated with the Roman church and all other branches of the Christian church. This church is past, present and future, but one church. It is the bride and the body of Christ, and He alone is its head. It is not, as some sects and branches of the church like to claim, a particular group within a denomination. God is not limited to such groups, and the church of Christ is not limited to such groups even though some people mistakenly convince themselves that this is so. The Presbyterian doctrine of the church as stated in the Confession, does not limit the invisible church to any visible branch of the church of Christ on the earth.

B. THE VISIBLE CHURCH

The Confession of Faith defines the visible church and its function in these words:

[80]

"The visible church, which is also catholic or universal under the gospel (not confined to one nation as before under the law), consists of all those throughout the world that profess the true religion, together with their children; and is the kingdom of the Lord Jesus Christ; the house and family of God, through which men are ordinarily saved and union with which is essential to their best growth and service." (Chapter XXVII, Article II).

1. INCLUDES ALL TRUE BELIEVERS IN CHRIST

Protestants sometimes ask, Does the church include members of the Roman church? This Presbyterian statement would suggest that all true believers in Christ, whatever their denomination, belong to the body of Christ. The church consists of all persons throughout the world that profess the true religion, together with their children. That much falsehood (from the point of view of the Bible as we understand it) is taught by Roman Catholics must be recognized. That neither we nor the Roman Catholics nor the members of other religious bodies who claim that no one can be saved except through membership with their particular group have the right to judge the faith of another should be underscored. God is the final judge. Presbyterians are committed to follow the teachings of the scriptures as faithfully as possible. They seek to bring others into the richer, larger faith that belongs to the children of God whenever and wherever they may do so.

2. INCLUDES MEMBERS OF OTHER EVANGELICAL CHURCHES

The reason why Presbyterians generally do seek converts from members of the Roman church is that these persons have been taught to believe that salvation is bestowed by the Roman church and we believe that salvation comes only through faith in Jesus Christ as Lord and Saviour. While it is true that the Christian Gospel is proclaimed by the church, it does not necessarily follow that men and women are saved by accepting the dogmas of the church. Presbyterians ordinarily receive letters of transfer from, and grant letters of transfer to, all leading evangelical church bodies. They likewise recognize the baptism of persons in such church bodies and do not re-baptize these persons as though their former baptism were invalid. These things are done because of the Presbyterian doctrine of the church, which includes all genuine believers in Christ, together with their children.

3. INCLUDES FELLOWSHIP WITH OTHER CHURCH BODIES

Can Presbyterians hold Christian fellowship with other bodies than their own? Most Presbyterians believe that they can. Some Presbyterians, in the interest of what they believe to be pure doctrine, are inclined to be more exclusive. The official statement in the Confession of Faith reads as follows:

"This catholic church has been sometimes more, sometimes less, visible. And particular churches, which are members thereof, are more or less pure, according as the doctrine of the gospel is taught and embraced, ordinances administered, and public worship performed more or less purely in them." (Chapter XXVII, Article IV.)

In most cases the touchstone of fellowship is the ministry of the sacraments (Baptism and the Lord's Supper) the word (the scriptures as the inspired rule of faith and life), and worship. These are considered necessary to the proper interpretation of the Gospel of Christ. It is the duty and the function of the church to use all of the means of God's appointment to convince and convert sinners, and to build them up in the most holy faith. While it is believed that the Presbyterian form of church government conforms most accurately to that indicated and taught in the scriptures, other forms of church government are recognized, and members following them are not excluded from the concept of the visible church.

Even though some churches and congregations have degenerated so as to become apparently not the churches of Christ, Presbyterians believe that "there shall always be a church on earth, to worship God according to His will." (Confession of Faith, Chapter XXVII, Article V.)

It is sometimes asked, Do the service agencies, such as those supported by Red Feather contributions, help to make up the church? Strictly speaking, they are not a part of the fellowship which, in a particular congregation, affirms its faith in Christ. But they serve as the outreaching arms of the church, just as Christian colleges, orphanages, hospitals, and other institutions do. They help to make up the Kingdom of God because they are motivated by, and largely supported by members of the visible church.

C. THE HEAD OF THE CHURCH

"The Lord Jesus Christ is the only head of the church, and the claim of any man to be the vicar of Christ and the head of the church, is without warrant in fact or in Scripture, even anti-Christian, a usurpation dishonoring to the Lord Jesus Christ." (Confession of Faith, Chapter XXVII, Article VI.)

This statement remains true to the New Testament doctrine of Christ as the head of the church. As was indicated in an earlier chapter, we believe that God by His Spirit made the scriptures our only rule of faith and life, and that no church or Council made them so. There were certain Councils which affirmed that the members of the church believed the scriptures of the Old and New Testaments to be the word of God. This was a declarative and not an authoritative pronouncement. The

Roman church claims to have made the Bible authoritative, and turns right around and makes the traditions of men more authoritative than the Bible. It has substituted a man elected by certain cardinals (who are human appointees) for Christ as head of the church. Presbyterians do not reject this practice in order to be contentious. They do so in order to be true to the scriptures and to let Christ remain the head of the church which He purchased with His own blood. They reject the usurpation of Christ's place by a man who holds to a tradition totally unwarranted in the scriptures.

It is because of a desire to prevent such usurpation that the Presbyterian church bodies elect moderators of Sessions, Presbyteries, Synods and Assemblies to serve for a specified time only. It is for this reason that Presbyterians constantly seek the guidance and power of the Holy Spirit, so that they might serve Christ the head of the church and accomplish His will in their service. For Christ, not a man or any group of men, is the sole head of the church which bears His name.

D. THE PLACE OF THE CHURCH IN GOD'S PLAN

Let us seek to discover the place of the church in God's plan of redemption as this is revealed in the Old Testament and the New Testament.

1. IN THE OLD TESTAMENT

The church as the organized body of believers in Christ does not appear as such in the Old Testament. However, as is indicated, for instance in Hebrews 11, there was a succession of the faithful who looked forward to the full realization of their faith in Him whom God would send. The New Testament witnesses to the fact that Jesus of Nazareth, Son of God and Son of man, is the one in whom that faith had full realization. The preaching of the book of Acts gives eloquent witness to this fact. The Old Testament prophets underscored the fact that the program of God would be accomplished, not through the unfaithful multitudes, but through a spiritual remnant of God's people. Paul in Romans, chapters 4 and 9, argues that the promises of God were to the spiritual rather than merely the physical seed of Abraham. Therefore the Old Testament people of God and the New Testament believers in Christ are one body in the sight of God.

In Jeremiah 31:31-34 we have an excellent statement of the fact that when the covenant people as a whole failed to claim their privileges under God, He would establish with them a new covenant written on their hearts. This covenant was realized partially in the remnant of the Hebrews that returned later from captivity, but more fully in the church established by Jesus Christ. Thus the Old Testament points toward the inwardness of the Kingdom of God, and the New Testament writers, following the teaching of Christ, see in Him the Messiah who would establish God's Kingdom, and in His church the spiritual flower of Old Testament Judaism. This proposition may be more clearly established by a recognition of the New Testament teaching concerning the church.

2. IN THE NEW TESTAMENT

The New Testament not only is rooted in the Old, but it clarifies the redemptive purpose of God in Jesus Christ and the church which He established to carry on His work in the world. According to Mark 3:14-15, Jesus chose and appointed the twelve "to be with him, and to be sent out to preach and have authority to cast out demons." He trained the twelve, together a larger number of believers, to carry on His work after His departure from the earth. He promised His presence and power to believers who would carry His Gospel into all the world. (See, for instance, Matthew 28:16-20 and Acts 1:8.) The book of Acts tells how they made a wonderful beginning in this task, and how they were enabled to witness through the power of His Spirit. Christ built His church on the conviction stated in Matthew 16:15-18, that He was the Messiah, the Son of the living God. The change from the use of the masculine gender, "Thou art Peter," to the neuter gender, "and on this rock" points to the conviction expressed by Peter and not to a person who claims the prerogatives of Christ. Believers in Christ went out to do the work committed to them by the head of the church. They were the branches of which He served as the vine. They were called to bear His fruit in the world, and they had His promise to be with them to the end of the world.

The New Testament letters present this same view of the place of the church in God's plan of redemption for the world. In I Corinthians 12 Paul presents the church as the body of Christ. In Ephesians 5:21-33 and Colossians 1:18-23, the church is the body of Christ of which He is the head and into which He pours His fulness. With all of its imperfections, the church is viewed as the body of Christ on the earth, the appointed fellowship to carry on His will in the world. Through it, as through the Old Testament Kingdom, God is working out His plan of redemption for mankind.

E. PRESBYTERIAN AND DISPENSATIONAL VIEWS OF THE CHURCH

A high doctrine of the church has been held by Presbyterians for many generations. However, in recent years another doctrine of the church has been embraced by some Presbyterians. The special type of premillenialism which serves as its rootage was advanced, as might be expected, by a person not in the Presbyterian tradition. His name was

John Darby, who founded and all but wrecked the early Church of the Plymouth Brethren. His doctrines in part have been accepted and developed into modern dispensationalism by one of the great Bible teachers of recent times, the late Dr. C. I. Scofield. It is natural for Presbyterians to feel the conflict between the dispensational views advanced by Dr. Scofield in his annotated Bible and the doctrines of historic Presbyterianism at certain points, for they stem from different points of view.

The question most frequently asked is stated in this form: Why is it that the Presbyterian church does not generally accept dispensationalism? The official reasons are stated in a pointed pamphlet which is the report of a special committee to the 1944 Assembly. This may be secured for five cents from a Presbyterian bookstore. It is not our purpose here to discuss all of the details of this report. Let us recognize some of the good points of persons who hold this type of theology and perhaps some of the reasons why Presbyterians as a whole do not recommend dispensationalism as a system of thought.

1. GOOD POINTS OF MANY DISPENSATIONALISTS

A great many Presbyterians who follow Dr. Scofield's seven dispensations (periods of time in which men are tested by a special revelation from God) are deeply spiritual persons. They are sincerely concerned about the church and its lack of spiritual vitality. They are evangelistic in spirit. They are very much interested in the study of the Bible. They have had an experience which gives them a zeal for God. Usually they are conservative in theology, desiring always to defend the faith which they believe was once for all delivered to the saints. Many of them are most loyal to the Presbyterian church and to their local pastor and congregation. It would therefore be very unfair to gather up all dispensationalists into one group and condemn them in the name of Presbyterianism. The Bible does not deliver itself on this subject, and neither do the Presbyterian Standards of our church. It is a theology and a movement which has developed since the Westminster Assembly of 1643 was called to meet.

2. BASIC DIFFERENCES BETWEEN DISPENSATIONALISM AND PRESBYTERIANISM

There are a few basic elements in dispensationalism as a theology which are at variance with the Presbyterian faith. One is the Presbyterian emphasis on salvation by faith alone as contrasted with the emphasis on testing (which at times is hard to distinguish from being saved) by different methods in different periods. The period under the law, for instance, is a period where, according to the New Testament, grace was also operative. Without the grace of God the Hebrews could not have been delivered from Egypt. Without God's grace the remnant could not have been saved after the captivity.

Another difference lies in the use of the term *dispensation*. Dr. Scofield divides all time into seven dispensations. Presbyterians believe in an Old Testament dispensation (which looks forward to the coming of Christ) and a New Testament dispensation (which recognizes Christ as having already come).

Still a third basic difference is the view of the sovereignty of God and the purpose of God in the two systems of thought. In dispensationalism the purpose of God is believed to center primarily in the Jewish people, and to have been thwarted when the Jews rejected Christ as Messiah. A quick change in plans instituted the church age, which is a sort of interlude before the renewal of God's purpose with His people, who are physical descendants of Abraham. The Jews are to be restored to a place of prominence at the return of Christ, which is believed to be imminent. Historic Presbyterianism refuses to surrender its belief in the sovereign purpose of God as having been made from all eternity. If God's purpose has to be changed when the Jews reject Christ, why not at any other time that man chooses to disobey God? Does not such a view weaken our view of God?

Again, while dispensationalism looks upon the church as a temporary and intermediary part of the secondary purpose of God, as already apostate and hardly worth saving, Presbyterians follow what they believe to be the New Testament teaching concerning the church as an integral and necessary part of God's plan from all eternity. They believe that Christ established the church to continue to witness and to do His work in the world. They believe that Paul was right in arguing in Romans 4 and 9 that the promises of God were intended for the spiritual seed of Abraham, and not merely for his physical seed. Therefore they view the predictions of Jesus concerning His suffering, death and resurrection as a part of the redemptive purpose of God, and the establishment of the church as the living witness to this redemptive purpose of God in Christ. Dispensationalists and Presbyterians agree that the church must witness, the former with more zeal than the latter. They differ as to the importance of the visible church in God's plan. Dispensationalists sometimes are divisive, putting their own understanding of Christian truth above loyalty to the local church or denomination. This is a part of the privilege of Protestantism, and is evident at times in other dispensational groups. But there is a basic difference between Presbyterian and dispensational theology concerning the place and the importance of the church in God's plan of redemption for the world.

Another difference between the Presbyterian Standards and dispensationalism is the emphasis on the present and the end of the world. Dispensationalism gives a much greater and more central place to the expected events associated with the return of Christ than does historic Presbyterianism. In dispensational thought, the return of Christ is expected to usher in a series of events which result in the physical restoration of the Jews to an earthly kingdom in Palestine, and in which the faithful saints who have been witnessing to Christ will be united with them in a rule with Christ for literally one thousand years. Many Presbyterians expect a rule of Christ for a thousand years after His return, but do not associate with this belief some of the other ideas advanced by dispensationalists. Other Presbyterians give greater emphasis to their task of striving to establish the Kingdom of God here and now, leaving to Christ the question of the consummation of events in the world by whatever pattern He chooses. Again we repeat that this difference is possible because there is no clear deliverance in the Presbyterian Standards on this subject. The Presbyterian church as a whole and the Presbyterian Standards give the emphasis to the ongoing obedience of God's people to His revealed will, not to a special series of events at the end of the present age. The belief in the return of Christ is clear and unmistakable, and Presbyterians hold this doctrine with all purpose and tenacity. But they may and do hold it without a system of events such as men have advanced in relation to this great and historic return. The Presbyterian teaching on this subject is set forth in a later chapter.

3. These Differences Lead to Different Interpretations of Scripture

All of these differences result from and lead to differences in interpretation of the scriptures. It is not, as some suppose, a difference in taking the scriptures literally or figuratively in two complete systems of thought. Dr. Scofield, for instance, is very literal when he interprets certain verses of the Revelation, chapter 20. He refuses to be literal in his interpretation of the messages to the churches in the same book, chapters 2 and 3. According to his teaching, the message to the church at Ephesus is not to the church at Ephesus, but to the church in a period of time that he has set. So also are all of the other messages. His system of thought determines where he will take passages literally and where he will take them figuratively. The same is true in part of Presbyterianism. However, as has been pointed out, Presbyterians reject certain dispensational doctrines because they are at variance with what they believe to be clear teachings of the scriptures in both the Old and the New Testaments as a whole, as well as specific teachings of Christ and the apostles. The difference is not one of judgment upon another set of ideas so much as it is one of loyalty to one's understanding of the scriptures.

4. The Purpose of this Presentation

It is to be hoped that this brief presentation of differences will bring greater understanding and harmony, and not greater misunderstanding and strife among Presbyterians. It should be pointed out that dispensational views are held to a greater or less extent by many who use the Scofield Reference Bible. Let Presbyterians learn from those who are more zealous and more spiritually concerned than they are. And let dispensationalists who are members of Presbyterian churches understand more clearly that the reason why ministers and others do not promote their doctrine more zealously is that they are loyal to the scriptures and the historic Presbyterian faith. Let both together become better witnesses to the saving power of Christ, to the doctrine of His abiding presence to guide and help, and to His ultimate return in His good time to consummate the redemptive work which has been going on for thousands of years.

F. THE RELATION OF CHRIST TO THE CHURCH

In the light of the discussion which has preceded, we may summarize the relation of Christ to the church in five statements:

1. Christ is the Saviour of believers in the church. He has always been the one through whom salvation comes. He will always serve this redemptive function.

2. Christ is the Lord and only head of the church. No intermediary or vicar was appointed by Him to take His place and none is needed to usurp His place in the church. He guides the church by the power of His Holy Spirit whenever and wherever the church is responsive to hear and to heed His voice.

3. Christ is related to the church as the vine is related to the branches or as the head is related to the body. He supplies the life, the power, the direction needed for the life, the growth, and the work of the church. The church commits itself to Him to carry out His directions as it draws daily strength from Him.

4. Christ is constantly working in and through the church in the person of the Holy Spirit. The promises of the book of Acts and the experiences described in the New Testament do not cease at the end of the first century. They belong to the church universal. They belong to us insofar as we will dare to claim them.

5. Christ will consummate the work of the church in the final judgment and will take all believers to the church triumphant in glory. The details are not all clear, but the truth shines through all the clouds of misunderstanding. He who has overcome the world will overcome the evil forces in the world and will claim His own forever.

As these statements indicate, Christ has the central and significant place in the life and thought of the church. Presbyterians are not ashamed to give Him His rightful place as Lord and head of the church which He purchased with His own blood.

G. THE MISSION OF THE CHURCH

The mission of the church is well stated in Matthew 28:16-20. The risen Lord sent out believers to make disciples of all nations. They were to do this by preaching the Gospel of redemption through Him who had become incarnate in the flesh, who had been crucified and raised for their redemption. These disciples were sent out to teach all that He had commanded them. The teaching which is now summarized in the Gospels and in the New Testament as a whole provides a rich content of Christian teaching. His instruction was to teach men to observe, to obey all that He had commanded. Thus the church which fulfills its mission must both preach to and teach all men. It is important to say, "Christ died for your redemption," but it is equally important to present every man mature in Christ through his deeper and wider understanding of the Christian faith. Presbyterians seek to obey this command by using all of the means of spiritual growth, including the proper observance of the two sacraments instituted by Christ. These means of growth will be discussed more fully in the next chapter.

The mission of the church is to do the work of Christ in the world until He comes. It is not sure when He will return, but is to remain faithfully at its task until that time. The church has the glorious mission of making Christ known, of proclaiming His Gospel and of applying it in all the relationships of life. To this mission the church may well consecrate itself day by day, week by week, month by month, year by year.

H. THE SOURCE OF POWER FOR THE CHURCH

The Holy Spirit brings to the believing church the power of God for its great task. The experiences described in the book of Acts reveal how ordinary and weak Christians were used in a remarkable way to make Christ known in a hostile world. In every age since that time the power of God has been offered to the church. The church has not always caught the vision of its Lord and has not always dared to claim His power to obey His command. Whenever it has become usable, it has received His power to obey. God's power is available to the church today. Let us study, pray, work, and obey that we may receive this power through the indwelling of the Holy Spirit. Then and then alone will the church march to accomplish its redemptive mission.

The high view of the church which is set forth in our Presbyterian Standards properly leads to a glorious experience of the power of God in the body of Christ. He longs to pour out His Spirit upon the church of the twentieth century. He longs to fill your church with the power it needs for a new obedience. Let us all become usable so that we may receive power in His name.

WORKSHEET

1. The invisible church is_____ _____
   _____

2. The visible church is_____ _____
   _____

3. Presbyterians believe that the keeping of the_____and the sacraments as Christ commanded are marks of the true church.

4. The only head of the church is_____ _____.

5. The church as a part of God's plan is revealed in_____ Testaments.

6. Dispensationalists may be commended for the following points even though their accepted system of thought differs in some respects from historic Presbyterianism:

   a.

   b.

   c.

7. Historic Presbyterianism and dispensationalism differ in emphasis on the following points:

   a.

   b.

   c.

   d.

8. Christ is related to the church as the_____is related to the
   _____.

9. The mission of the church is_____
   _____

10. The church receives its power from the indwelling of the_____
    _____.

11. I would like to have further discussion of:

    a.

    b.

CHAPTER IX

Our Means of Spiritual Growth

INTRODUCTION

In the chapters that precede, we have established the fundamental principle that salvation is by faith in Jesus Christ. No amount of works, however good they may be, are able to bring us into an experience of salvation. Yet no person can be saved without being saved to serve. That is to say, we are saved *from* sin *to* a life of service.

This life of service requires the constant use of the means of growth appointed by God and revealed in the scriptures. We propose to consider these means of growth in this chapter. As we do so, let us keep in mind the fundamental proposition that while redemption is provided once for all in Jesus Christ, the Lord and Saviour of believers, redemption is applied day by day to believers through the activity of the Holy Spirit. The Holy Spirit ordinarily works through the means of grace with which we shall be concerned.

A. OBEDIENCE TO THE LAW OF GOD

By the law of God is meant not only the Ten Commandments of the Old Testament re-interpreted by the New Testament law of love, but also the whole revealed will of God. The large place given to the Ten Commandments in the Catechisms of our church reflects both the importance of obedience to the law of God and the training of John Calvin as a lawyer before he became a great reformer.

The importance of obedience to the revealed will of God is well stated by James 2:18: "But some one will say, 'You have faith and I have works.' Show me your faith apart from your works, and I by my works will show you my faith." The way one lives reveals the quality of one's faith. When the Apostle Paul received his heavenly vision, he responded in obedience. That obedience became the secret both of learning the Father's will and of gaining power to do it.

A servant in the far east was observed to anticipate the slightest wish of her mistress. When asked how she became so adept at her task, she replied: "I made up my mind to obey every wish of my mistress immediately. By doing this I learned to anticipate her wishes so that she seldom has to express them to me."

Believers who obey as perfectly as they can, come into a rich fellowship with God. They understand His will better and they gain power to do it. Thus they grow spiritually. Paul stated the principle well in his letter to the Philippians: "Work out your own salvation with fear and trembling; for God is at work in you, both to will and to work for his good pleasure." (Philippians 2:12, 13) Because he realized the relationship between believing and doing, Paul usually devoted the first part of his letters to doctrine and the latter part to an appeal to right conduct. Protestants who know that they are saved by faith and not by works also accept the words of Paul to the Ephesians: "For we are his workmanship, created in Christ Jesus for good works, which God prepared beforehand, that we should walk in them." (Ephesians 2:10).

It is not too much to say that the believer can have only a stunted growth if he does not learn to obey the will of God. It has also been proved by the saints of the church that God works in us *as* we obey, not apart from our faith put to work.

B.   CHRISTIAN EDUCATION

After the long night of ignorance which marked the Dark Ages, the Renaissance period in European history issued in a new zest for learning. However, this learning did not extend to the common people. Luther made an appeal to the common people through the German Bible and his various tracts. Because of the doctrine of the priesthood of believers, which made every man a priest before God without the aid of the intermediaries of the Roman church, Luther felt that believers should be educated. They should have the Bible in their own tongue and they should be instructed in the doctrines and principles of the Christian religion.

Even moreso than Luther, John Calvin established in Geneva a school of religion without an equal on the continent. To this center came Protestant leaders from Europe and the British Isles. Among the more famous of his pupils was John Knox, who brought the Reformation to Scotland and hence in part to America. But Calvin set out also to instruct the people of Geneva who lacked the training which made John Knox the great preacher he became. Presbyterians have believed in education throughout their history, for they believe that every man should search the will of God for his life and that every man should be well informed concerning the principles of our holy religion.

For Presbyterians, Christian education is centered in the Bible and its teachings. Calvin's sermons are expositions of the scriptures. His *Institutes of the Christian Religion* are an effort to systematize the theology taught in the scriptures. The Confession of Faith and the Catechisms make full use of the scriptures and provide footnotes which give scriptural references for every doctrine presented. These doctrines are either clearly set forth in scripture or may logically be deduced therefrom.

Presbyterians therefore believe, not only in Higher Education, but in the education of each child, each young person, each adult in the Christian faith. They believe that the church and the home are allies in the educational work of the church. In more recent years they have sought to adapt Christian truth to the understanding of children and youth at the various age levels. They propose to develop lay leaders who will be able to do a significant job of teaching. In many cases Presbyterians are taking the lead in developing new techniques and new materials to make education more effective at the local church level.

Presbyterians take seriously the injunction of Paul to Timothy: "Do your best to present yourself to God as one approved, a workman who has no need to be ashamed, rightly handling the word of truth." (II Tim. 2:15). They believe that spiritual growth comes through an understanding of the word of God and the will of God. The Holy Spirit uses the word in a remarkable way to convert sinners and to build them up in our most holy faith. Thus Christian education becomes a vital and essential means of spiritual growth.

C. PRAYER AND WORSHIP

From the time that Jesus taught His disciples to pray, prayer has been at the very heart of Christian worship and Christian growth. Prayer is one form of worship. It brings believers into fellowship and communion with God. Prayer is listening for the voice of God. Worship is ascribing glory to God. The Shorter Catechism defines prayer in this way: "Prayer is an offering up of our desires unto God, for things agreeable to his will, in the name of Christ, with confession of our sins, and thankful acknowledgment of his mercies." (Answer to Ques. 98.) The Larger Catechism adds one important phrase, "by the help of His Spirit" (Ans. 178). Such prayer as a part of the worship of God may be both private and public.

1. PRIVATE PRAYER AND WORSHIP

Presbyterians believe that private and family worship are very important. For this reason they have prepared devotional booklets for young people (Thy Will, My Will) and for adults (Day by Day). A great many other books and pamphlets are also available for use. Family altars are encouraged as a means of developing spiritual growth. The reading of the word of God, the learning and quoting of favorite verses and passages, the singing of psalms and hymns, and the habit of praying in family groups are encouraged. Christians are also encouraged to have their own private devotions. For worship is a very personal experience with God. Prayer is a very intimate way of keeping in tune with God and in fellowship with Him. The various forms of private and family worship are means of discovering the will of God, of being inspired by His presence, and of being strengthened by His power. No specific rules are laid down as to how long or how frequently one should engage in private or family worship. Daily worship which issues in a conscious walk with God through every hour of the day is believed to be essential for the greatest spiritual growth.

2. PUBLIC WORSHIP

Public Worship ordinarily consists of recognizing and sanctifying the sabbath day as a special day of worship; of assembling as a congregation for divine worship; of the public reading of the holy scriptures; of the singing of psalms and hymns; of bringing an offering to God; of pubic prayer; and of the preaching of the word. At stated intervals it also consists of the administering of the two sacraments, Baptism and the Lord's Supper.

A. SANCTIFYING THE SABBATH DAY

Even though the pressure and the customs of modern life tend to make the Sabbath a holiday rather than a holy day, the Presbyterian Confession of Faith is explicit in its statements concerned the Sabbath. It says:

"As it is of the law of nature that, in general, a due proportion of time be set apart for the worship of God; so, in his word, by a positive, moral, and perpetual commandment, binding all men in all ages, he hath particularly appointed one day in seven for a Sabbath, to be kept holy unto him: which, from the beginning of the world to the resurrection of Christ, was the last day of the week; and from the resurrection of Christ, was changed into the first day of the week, which in scripture is called the Lord's day, and is to be continued to the end of the world as the Christian Sabbath." Ch. XXIII, Art. VII.

Let us make a few pertinent observations about this statement. First, while nature and human history teach the importance of setting apart one day in seven for the worship of God, He has expressly commanded in scripture the Sabbath to be kept holy unto Himself. The question is not, as some suppose, a question whether or not they choose to keep the Sabbath. It is rather a question of what God commands. Frenchmen tried to destroy the Sabbath during the French Revolution. They did not destroy the Sabbath. They rather sowed the seeds of decay which led to the degeneration and the decline of France as a leading nation in Europe and the world. Let history speak to men and women in the present. The more big meetings and big deals we have on the Sabbath, the more sure we are to lose our keen moral sense and our sense of destiny under God. We cannot break the Sabbath law of God. We may ignore it until it breaks us.

[94]

A second observation is that the resurrection of Jesus Christ is such a significant act of redemption that Christians observe the first day of the week rather than the seventh as the Sabbath. He began the new day and the new life for believers. The power of the resurrection may well be reclaimed by Presbyterians as they worship on the Lord's day.

Our Confession also defines the way in which the Sabbath is to be kept in these words:

"This Sabbath is then kept holy unto the Lord when men, after a due preparing of their hearts, and ordering of their common affairs beforehand, do not only observe an holy rest all the day from their own works, words, and thoughts about their worldly employments and recreations; but also are taken up the whole time in public and private exercises of his worship, and in the duties of necessity and mercy." Ch. XXIII, Art. VIII.

The proper observance of the Sabbath requires preparation on Saturday. The excuse that one is too tired to worship after a wild party Saturday night reveals a complete lack of understanding of this requirement. Just as one orders his business and plans for a vacation trip, so he is to plan for the proper observance of the Sabbath. The proper observance of the Sabbath requires also a holy rest from regular labors. It is true that some persons are required by necessity to work on the Sabbath. This is true of ministers and others who find the Sabbath one of their hardest days. Yet even in their work they are drawn very close to God in worship, and this makes the day different from any other. Others who labor may likewise find a day off each week when they can be refreshed in body, mind and spirit.

Furthermore, the proper observance of the Sabbath, in addition to preparation and holy rest, requires public and private worship, together with works of necessity and mercy. The human soul requires feeding just as surely as does the human body. It requires regular inspiration, study and exercise for its highest spiritual growth. This is why regular periods of worship are essential, just as they were essential for our Lord while He was on earth. This is why the Presbyterian Standards set forth the teachings of scripture on the highly important subject of Sabbath observance. If we have slipped concerning the Sabbath, let us re-examine our motives, our attitudes and our habits to bring them more nearly into line with the teachings of our rule of faith and life.

B. WORSHIPING GOD IN HIS SANCTUARY

The first principle which governs the worship of God is that God must be worshiped according to His revealed will and not according to the devices of men. This means that He is not to be worshiped in any way not prescribed in holy scripture. (See the Confession of Faith, Chapter XXIII for these requirements.)

The second principle is that the Triune God alone is to be worshiped. Neither angels, nor saints, nor any other creatures are to be worshiped (or venerated). All worship is to come, not through human mediators, but through Jesus Christ, the great High Priest of the Christian church.

Prayer with thanksgiving is required of all. Such prayer, offered in genuine humility through the help of the Holy Spirit, is to be made in and through Jesus Christ. It is to be offered fervently in faith, love, and perseverance. If it is vocal, it is to be offered in a known tongue. Our Confession states further:

"Prayer is to be made for things lawful, and for all sorts of men living, or that shall live hereafter; but not for the dead." (Chapter XXIII, Article IV.)

Prayer and the other forms of worship are not limited by time or place. God is to be worshiped in spirit and in truth at all times and everywhere that such worship may be forthcoming.

The *scriptures* have a large place in public worship. They are to be read with reverence and godly fear. They are to be heard "in obedience unto God with understanding, faith, and reverence." The preaching is to be an exposition of the truth of the Bible and its application to the life of men. The pulpit in Presbyterianism is not to be regarded as a sounding board for the opinions of men, but a flaming altar for the proclamation of the Gospel of God. This Gospel is set forth in all its clarity and power in the word of God, and is applied by the Holy Spirit to believers through the preaching of that word.

From the time that the Hebrews brought their gifts to build the tabernacle, the scriptures set forth the privilege and the duty of *giving* as a means of worship and spiritual growth. Through the worship of giving men and women, boys and girls are made partners with God in the work of His Kingdom on the earth.

The "*singing* of psalms with grace in the heart" is another part of public worship. It is good to praise God with the heart and with the lips. The whole congregation is brought more closely into fellowship with God through the singing of psalms and hymns.

The proper administration and the worthy receiving of *the sacraments* is another part of worship. This is occasional rather than weekly, but it has its proper place in regular worship. More will be said about the sacraments a little later. It is sufficient to say that the public worship of God is necessary to one's spiritual growth. One may worship in isolation, but usually one has a richer experience in the public worship of

God. Presbyterians believe that both private and public worship supplement each other as means of spiritual growth. The Presbyterian Directory for Worship offers practical suggestions for making all of the parts of public worship more meaningful. (See the Directory for Worship, chapters I-VII.)

D. THE SACRAMENTS

Mention has been made of the proper observance of the sacraments as means of spiritual growth. By definition, "sacraments are holy signs and seals of the covenant of grace, immediately instituted by God, to represent Christ and his benefits, and to confirm our interest in Him: as also to put a visible difference between those that belong unto the church, and the rest of the world; and solemnly to engage them to the service of God in Christ, according to His word." (Confession of Faith, Chapter XXIX, Article II. See this chapter as a whole.)

Presbyterians do not believe that sacraments in themselves or the elements used have any magic about them. The visible sign of water used in baptism is a symbol of the cleansing power of God's Spirit. The bread and the wine used in the Lord's Supper are likewise symbols representing the body and blood of Christ. The important thing is the spiritual relationship which exists between the believer and God. This relationship was pictured by Jesus as a vine-branch relationship. Spiritual feeding upon His life is a symbolized and encouraged in the sacrament of the Lord's Supper. While the sacraments must be properly administered according to the teaching of the word of God, they are not ends in themselves, but means of bringing believers into a more vital and meaningful relationship with God through Christ.

1. WHY PRESBYTERIANS OBSERVE ONLY TWO SACRAMENTS

The reason why Presbyterians observe only two sacraments is that there were only two ordained by Christ. The other five observed by the Roman church were developed as a part of their tradition. Our Confession says:

"There be only two sacraments ordained by Christ our Lord in the gospel, that is to say, baptism and the supper of the Lord: neither of which may be dispensed by any but by a minister of the word, lawfully ordained." (Confession of Faith, Chapter XXIX, Article IV.)

2. THE SACRAMENT OF BAPTISM

Baptism is administered to believers who are admitted to membership in the church and are to each believer "a sign and seal of the covenant of grace, of his ingrafting into Christ, of regeneration, of remission of sins, and of his giving up unto God, through Jesus Christ, to walk in newness of life." (Chapter XXX, Article I.) It is also administered to the infants of one or both believing parents. In the case of infants, parents are required to renew their vows as Christians, and to covenant before God and the church that they will train ·their children in the Christian faith, pray with and for them, set before them a godly example, and encourage them in every way to become Christians when they reach the age of their own decision.

Presbyterians do not believe that immersion is necessary, but that pouring or sprinkling water upon the person is sufficient. They do not forbid immersion. The form is not considered the essential thing in baptism, but the inner and spiritual meaning. What is promised by parents of children and what is experienced by youth or adults in the cleansing power of God's Spirit are considered essential to the spiritual growth of believers in baptism.

3. The Sacrament of the Lord's Supper

Ordinarily the Lord's Supper is observed at least once a quarter. It may be observed as often as a Session sees fit to schedule it. The words of institution, a prayer of consecration, a meditation calling for sincere self-examination, reverent partaking of the elements by faith, and the singing of a hymn characterize the observance of this sacrament. It is designed to renew the faith and the life of the participants and to send them forth strengthened for the duties and the privileges of Christian service. Presbyterians recognize that this is the Lord's table and invite all other evangelical Protestants to partake with them. In like manner they recognize the baptism of evangelical Protestant churches and do not require that all adults be re-baptized.*

These two sacraments have proved to be of great value in spiritual growth, and are held in high honor by members of the Presbyterian church.

E. THE COMMUNION OF SAINTS

By *saints* Presbyterians mean sinners saved by grace who are becoming more and more like Christ. They do not mean persons who have been named saints by some official action of a church. Saints are bound together in two ways. They are bound to Christ the head of the church and they are bound to one another as members of the family of God. Their communion with Christ does not make them equal with Christ but makes them more like Christ. Their communion with one another does not take away the personality or property rights of any individual. We

---

*For a fuller interpretation of the meaning of the Lord's Supper, see the author's "How to Study I Corinthians," pp. 82-91.

have already discussed in this chapter some of the ways in which believers may commune with Christ. Let us recognize also the communion of saints with one another. The Confession says:

> "Saints by their profession are bound to maintain an holy fellowship and communion in the worship of God, and in performing such other spiritual services as tend to their mutual edification; as also in relieving each other in outward things, according to their several abilities and necessities. Which communion, as God offereth opportunity, is to be extended unto all who, in every place, call upon the name of the Lord Jesus." (Ch. XXVIII, Art. II.)

A Presbyterian congregation is not a social club which may be maintained and supported or disbanded and destroyed at will. It is a holy fellowship of believers. Such believers, because they are bound together in the family of God, are to worship and perform other spiritual services that build them up in the faith. As they are able, they are required to relieve one another in outward things. They are also expected to extend the right hand of fellowship to all who call upon the name of the Lord Jesus. There is no place for a divisive spirit in Presbyterianism. Presbyterians stand for something important in faith and conduct. Let them not compromise their high position. But let them also know that they are not to become Pharisaic and proud of their theology to a point where they become un-Christian in attitude or conduct. For while Presbyterians belong to a particular branch of the Christian church, they belong also to the church of Christ which far exceeds the bounds and the membership of their own denomination. This is not to argue for or against union with other bodies. It is to state the principle of the Confession that the Body of Christ is greater than our own particular denomination.

The means of growth in which Presbyterians believe have not all been treated in this chapter. No one of them has been treated adequately. Yet perhaps the readers have been stimulated to study the Confession, the Catechisms, and the Directory for Worship more carefully. If this has been done, it may yield rich fruits in the life of the church.

WORKSHEET

1. In an earlier chapter we have established the principle that salvation is by_____alone.

2. We recognize as a fundamental fact that while redemption is provided once for all in Jesus Christ, it is constantly being applied to believers by the_____ _____.

3. Obedience to the will of God is an important means of growth because:

   a.

   b.

4. For Presbyterians Christian education centers in the_____ and its_____.

5. Prayer is _____.

6. Worship is _____.

7. Presbyterians believe in keeping the_____as a holy day. In order to keep this day for rest and worship and service, it is necessary to_____for it on Saturday.

8. Public worship has several parts. Among these are: a._____ b._____ c._____ d._____

9. Presbyterians believe that only two sacraments were instituted by Christ. These two are_____and the_____ _____.

10. Presbyterians believe in the communion of saints. By saints they mean _____.

11. All of the above are means of_____ _____and are to be cultivated reverently and faithfully.

12. I would like to have a further discussion of:

    a.

    b.

CHAPTER X

Our Task in the Home

INTRODUCTION

Our Confession does not say a great deal about the Christian home. Its treatment for the most part comes out in the instruction concerning worship, the sacrament of Baptism, and the section on Marriage and Divorce. The Presbyterian Directory for Worship is very explicit concerning the duty of parents in the home. Of course, our standards point always to the Bible, where a good deal is revealed about the task of parents in the home. From these sources let us recognize what at least many Presbyterians believe concerning our task in the home.

A. PREPARING TO ESTABLISH CHRISTIAN HOMES

Christian homes are not accidents. They are the result of much prayer, careful planning, and persistent effort. Their purpose is to provide for the procreation of the race, for mutual helpfulness of husband and wife, and for the spiritual growth of all members of the home. A home is heaven in miniature. It therefore becomes important for Presbyterians and all others to prepare for Christian home-making.

In recent years Presbyterians have become more aware of the importance of training young people to approach marriage with the proper purposes and attitudes. The meaning of love at its deepest and highest levels, the importance of similar social and religious backgrounds for those to be married, the sacredness of the marriage relationship, the necessity of mutual understanding and regular worship, the dangers of petting and lax relationships between the sexes are among the topics being considered by youth groups in Presbyterian churches. Likewise the reasons for discouraging marriage between Christians and non-Christians, Protestants and Roman Catholics are carefully considered. All of this is reinforced and buttressed by teaching in the home wherever parents take their responsibility seriously.

Such efforts as have been described are an effort to live within the statement of our Confession in Chapter XXVI, Article III, which says:

> "It is lawful for all sorts of people to marry who are able with judgment to give their consent, yet it is the duty of Christians to marry only in the Lord. And, therefore, such as profess the true reformed religion should not marry with infidels, Romanists, or any idolaters; neither should such as are godly be unequally yoked by marrying with such as are notoriously wicked in their life, or maintain dangerous heresies."

As a further means of preparing for Christian marriage, many ministers insist upon one or more conferences with prospective brides and grooms in order to help them to understand more clearly the importance of a Christian home and to urge them to consecrate themselves more purposefully to establish and maintain a Christian home. Presbyterians at their best believe in preparing to make one's home a Christian home in every sense of the word.

B. FAMILY WORSHIP, EXAMPLE AND TEACHING

The privilege and duty of parents is well summarized in the vows which are taken at the baptism of their infants. Not only are they reminded of their child's need of the cleansing blood of Jesus Christ and of a saving faith in Him, but they are also asked to affirm:

"Do you now unreservedly dedicate your child to God, and promise, in humble reliance upon divine grace, that you will endeavor to set before (him) a godly example, that you will pray with and for (him), that you will teach (him) the doctrines of our holy religion, and that you will strive, by all the means of God's appointment, to bring (him) up in the nurture and admonition of the Lord?" (Book of Church Order, page 185.)

1. THE VOWS OF PARENTS

Parents who take these vows promise to pray with and for their children. The normal means by which family prayers are maintained is called regular family worship. The reading and recitation of portions of scripture, the use of devotional aids, the singing of hymns, and the offering of prayers are recommended ways of worshiping God in the family. Some families add more serious study to the usual forms of reading. The prayers of parents for children and the prayers of children for their own growth in grace are means of maintaining Christian homes. If there are parents who have not lived up to their vows, let them bring their habits into line with their purposes. They have the grace of God offered for this exercise if they will only take that grace and use it. Ministers will be glad to help any parents who desire to make a start in this direction.

These vows also require that parents set a godly example before their children. The claim that Christ is able to transform our lives becomes an idle claim unless and until it is demonstrated to some degree in our lives. Children need not be expected to take the Christian religion seriously unless their parents do. The power of example is the strongest power known to children. Whatever the temptations of parents, they should be fully aware that their weaknesses may well prove to be the undoing of their children.

David, for instance, took Uriah's wife and had him killed in battle. His son Solomon magnified this weakness (in the public interest, of course) until he had 700 wives and 300 concubines. Solomon's son Rehoboam (David's grandson) insisted on keeping this harem and adding to it at public expense so that the Kingdom was divided permanently, with only two tribes left for Rehoboam to rule over. No matter what David might have said to Solomon, his example was greater than his words, and the consequences of his weakness reached out into the national life of his people.

The secret sins of parents sometimes prevent them from striving for high ideals in the lives of their children. So the secret sins come out in loss of purpose and ideals even though they may not be known for a long time to the children. The children inherit the consequences even though they do not know the specific sins of their parents. To the beasts of the field God gives the power of procreation. To parents He also gives the task of living abundantly before their children.

These vows likewise call for Christian teaching. Even though the most powerful teaching is that of example, other teaching is necessary. The scriptures of the Old and New Testaments, the doctrines of our holy religion which are summarized in the Standards in which these studies center, and the other means of spiritual growth to which reference has been made provide rich teaching materials for alert parents. While it is true that Presbyterians require for membership only repentance from sin, faith in Christ, a desire after a new obedience and a purpose to support the life and work of a Christian church, it is also true that the vows which Presbyterian parents take require a great deal more than these things.

2. The Teaching Responsibility of the Home

The teaching of the Catechisms has somewhat gone out of style in many homes. One reason for this is that too much of the task of parents was turned over to the church school and there was not sufficient time to do all that needed to be done. Another is that current educational methods strive for understanding of memory work, not mere memorizing alone. Still another is that the wording of the Shorter Catechism is not designed for children or youth. Whatever the reasons may be, the net consequence is that we have produced a generation of Presbyterians who do not know much about the doctrines of our holy religion. This course of study is one of several efforts designed to help meet the present need. For we cannot do without a theology any more than we can do without an engine under the hood of an automobile.

While therefore the church has a teaching obligation to its members, the church also must encourage persons in the home to fulfill the vows that they have taken before God and many witnesses. Our task in the home is a teaching task in which, by precept and example, we strive by all the means of God's appointment, to rear children "in the nurture and admonition of the Lord." This teaching is designed to help children, when they come to the age of decision, to choose Christ as Lord and Saviour, and to commit their lives to Him in worship and in service.

It should be recognized that many parents will have disappointments in the response of their children to Christian teaching and example. This is much more frequent and much more trying when only one parent is carrying the responsibility which belongs to two. It is even more heartbreaking when the influence of one parent is negative or antagonistic. Let those who strive remember that the grace of Christ is sufficient for our every need, and that often we are chastened for our own spiritual growth. When your heart is perfect toward God and when you have done all that you can, leave the results with Him who is more concerned even than you are over those whom you love.

Let us be proud of the fact that Presbyterians believe in the responsibility of parents. For parents are God's partners, commissioned by Him to be the instruments through whom He works in the lives of those they love. They have a glorious privilege and a solemn responsibility.

C. THE RELATION BETWEEN PARENTS AND CHILDREN

This relationship is best described by the Apostle Paul in Ephesians 6:1-4. The first requirement of children is that they obey parents in the Lord. Parents should always be careful, therefore, to be in the Lord. Then they will merit the respect which is due to them.

The promise made to those who honor their parents in the Lord is that it will be well with them and that they will live long on the earth. This promise should not be taken to mean that eighty-five years is promised to every child who obeys his parents. It does mean that this is best for the home and for society in the long run. Children may honor their parents most by living a godly life through the power of Christ.

Fathers are enjoined not to provoke their children to anger or exasperation. This means that parents must exercise self-discipline if they expect to exercise discipline over their children. The self-discipline is basic to the discipline. Parents sometimes forget this important fact. They stand for God to their children in the sense that they represent authority and justice and love. Let every man who says he loves God teach children that God is love. And let this redemptive love be expressed in its components of justice and mercy. Let it have a redemptive purpose in the lives of children.

Fathers (and mothers as well) are to bring their children up in the nurture and admonition of the Lord. Christian nurture belongs to the home just as surely as does physical nurture. Providing food and clothing for the body, and developing tact and skill in relationships with other members of society are a part of the physical and social nurture of children. But these are not enough. Training children in godliness is also the duty of parents. It is their highest and most solemn duty. The instruction to which reference was made in this chapter is a part of this training. By prayer, by example, and by teaching, parents are able to discharge this obligation to their children.

A Christian home is a little bit of heaven on earth, but it must be made so by the power of the God of heaven. It is the most permanent, the most universal, and the most effective school of Christ in the world. But it must be made so in order to be so. This is why the relationship between parents and children in the home is so important. Children bring out the qualities of self-discipline and sacrificial love in parents. Parents teach children the Christian way of living. Together they form the home in which God dwells among His people.

D. THE CHURCH AND THE HOME AS ALLIES

Just as the Christian home supports the life and work of the church, the church seeks to maintain the Christian home. The two are mutually dependent. Families from homes make up the church family.

1. HELPING TO PROTECT THE SACREDNESS OF MARRIAGE

One of the ways the church helps to maintain the home is through its regulations concerning marriage. It does not deny the civil right to marriage. It encourages marriage by a minister of the church. Furthermore, in addition to its training in preparation for marriage and for the perpetuation of the home as a center for spiritual growth, the church strives to maintain the home by permitting only one ground for divorce. The statement of the Confession on this matter is as follows:

"Adultery or fornication, committed after a contract, being detected before marriage, giveth just occasion to the innocent party to dissolve that contract. In the case of adultery after marriage, it is lawful for the innocent party to sue out a divorce, and after the divorce to marry another, as if the offending party were dead." (Chapter XXVI, Article V.)

Following studies of the problem of divorce and re-marriage, the General Assembly of the Presbyterian Church, U.S. in 1959 amended the Directory for Worship, particularly paragraph 376, to allow for the re-marriage of some divorced persons where genuine repentance and a new purpose were evident. The Christian Church has a ministry to all who have sinned as well as to all who have kept their lives pure. Without its high ideals home life may easily disintegrate. For this reason it must protect the home in every way possible.

2. COOPERATING IN CHRISTIAN EDUCATION AND SERVICE

The church and the home are allies in Christian education and service. Home preparation for the learning experience of the church school, so long neglected by many Presbyterians, is beginning to be emphasized once more. The example of parents in piety and consistent living before children, as encouraged by the church, makes these two agencies of redemption one in purpose and activity. A clear statement of the duties of parents in religious education is contained in the Directory for Worship, Chapter XVII, paragraph 393:

> "In the supreme task of religious education, parents should cooperate with the church by setting their children an example in regular and punctual attendance upon the sessions of the church school and the services of the sanctuary, by assisting them in the preparation of their lessons, and by leading them in the consistent application of the teachings of the Gospel in their daily lives."

From the above statements and discussion it is apparent that our Standards do set forth the fundamental principles on which Presbyterians strive to build a strong home life among their members.

WORKSHEET

1. Our Confession does not say a great deal about the_____
_____. However, this does not mean that Presbyterians consider the home unimportant.

2. Christian homes result from_____, _____,
and _____.

3. It is the duty of Christians to marry only_____ _____.
It is dangerous for Presbyterians to marry_____,
_____, or_____.

4. Parents who have children baptized promise, in humble reliance upon divine grace, to set before their child a_____ _____,
to_____with and for him (or her), to_____him (or her) the doctrines of our holy religion, and to strive, by all the means of God's appointment, to bring him (or her) up in the
_____and_____of the Lord.

[106]

5. Parents are thus required to be careful of both their_____ and their_____.

6. The relation between parents and children requires the exercise of _____in love and obedience with_____.

7. The church and the home are_____in Christian nurture.

8. As a result of thinking through this chapter, I am resolved that I will:

    a.

    b.

9. I would like to have a further discussion of the following topics:

    a.

    b.

CHAPTER XI

Our Task in Society

The teaching of our Standards concerning our task in society is not treated under this topic. There is a body of teaching given in relation to the last six commandments and the second petition in the Lord's Prayer. These are brought together in conjunction with passages of scripture which throw light on this topic.

A. THE INDIVIDUAL AND SOCIETY

In the treatment of the visible and the invisible church, it was recognized that the visible church is in a society of men on the earth. Because it is in such a society, and because its members are members also of society, the church visible is more or less pure. Any individual believer may be pure in heart through the grace and power of Christ. Salvation is an individual matter. Yet men ordinarily are saved through the church. Their union with the church is essential to their best growth and service.

These concepts underlie the fundamental principle that Christian believers are both separate from society and a part of society. They are separate from unbelieving society in that they are called out by the grace of God. They are in society in that they are sent to the world to bring Christ to it. The same Jesus who said to His disciples, "Come ye after me" also said, "Go ye into all the world." Thus the individual is directly related to God through Christ. He is in a fellowship of like persons who exercise a saving faith, and in this fellowship is strengthened by his worship and service. He is also a citizen of his total society, a large part of which needs the redemptive power of God through Christ. He thus becomes a missionary, an evangelist, a reformer, a person who strives to bring the power and light of the Gospel of Christ to his world.

B. THE WORK OF CALVIN IN GENEVA

The principle of separation between church and state is an excellent principle as it was conceived by our founding fathers. History demonstrates the fact that state support of the church tends to mean and usually means state control of the church. Witness what has happened in Germany and Russia in recent years. At the same time there is a moral obligation on the church to help the state become a better state and the world a better world. In John Calvin's time in Switzerland this latter principle was in operation even though the principle of separation was not. So John Calvin returned to Geneva and went about reforming both the church and the city. He found all of his basic principles in the Bible. His rules of discipline were applied to both the church and the city.

The reforms in Genevan society are described in this way by an eminent historian:

"The material prosperity of the city was not neglected. Greater cleanliness was introduced, which is next to Godliness, and promotes it. Calvin insisted upon the removal of filth from houses and the narrow and crowded streets. He induced the magistrates to super- intend the markets, and to prevent the sale of unhealthy food, which was to be cast into the Rhone. Low taverns and drinking shops were abolished, and intemperance diminished. Mendicancy in the streets was prohibited. A hospital and poorhouse were provided and well- conducted. Efforts were made to give useful employment to every man who could work. Altogether Geneva owes her moral and temporal prosperity, her intellectual and literary activity, her social refinement, and her world-wide fame very largely to the reformation and discipline of Calvin. He set a high and noble example of a model community."

(Quoted by Walter Lingle, *Presbyterians, Their History and Beliefs,* p. 32.)

It is quite obvious that the Presbyterian church would not attempt to exercise a similar control over the civil life of a city or community. At the same time Presbyterians recognize the fact that they have a Gos- pel which transforms civic leaders and society insofar as it is voluntarily received and put to work. This fact leads us to recognize the possibili- ties open to us for the transformation of society by the Gospel of Jesus Christ.

C. THE TRANSFORMATION OF SOCIETY BY THE GOSPEL

The last six commandments forbid lack of respect for parents, murder, adultery, dishonesty, false accusation, and covetousness. All of these rear their ugly heads in our society. The God who forbids the practice of these things also provides the way that they may be over- come; namely, through the Christian Gospel.

Christians pray that God's Kingdom may come, that His will may be done on earth as it is in heaven. God's Kingdom comes on the earth through the obedience of God's people. And Jesus Christ said, "Go therefore and make disciples of all nations, baptizing them in the name of the Father and of the Son and of the Holy Spirit, teaching them to observe all that I have commanded you; and lo, I am with you always, to the close of the age." (Matthew 28:19, 20.)

Because some people in our world have exercised a social concern without identifying themselves as believers in Christ as Son of God and

Saviour of the world, many Christians have drawn back from the task of making our society more Christian. They have assumed that there is a distinction to be drawn between a "personal" Gospel and a "social" Gospel. This unrealistic error limits the power of Christ and runs counter to Jesus' example of healing sick bodies and feeding hungry stomachs. He said, "As you did it unto one of the least of these my brethren, you did it unto me." (Matthew 25:40.) The more we recognize the power of Christ's Gospel, the more convinced we will be that it will make a change in our world. Let us therefore recognize how this power of the Gospel works.

1. THROUGH TRANSFORMED INDIVIDUALS

In previous studies we have recognized the fact that salvation is a very personal experience. It brings an individual into a vital and transforming relationship with Jesus Christ as Lord and Saviour. We have also underscored the importance of the Christian fellowship as a transforming fellowship. Christians in fellowship enrich both individual and group experience. The influence of one Christian over another is one of the means by which the total experience of redemption is made more effective.

The first step toward transforming society is therefore the step of evangelizing and converting individuals in society. The effective proclamation of the Christian Gospel is the church's primary business. God's Spirit has a way of using this proclamation of the Gospel for the redemption of men. However, this witnessing to the power of God is not limited to the pulpit. Business men and women, employers and employees may witness by the way they operate in business more effectively than they do by their words in religious meetings. For this reason the church can never stop with the profession of faith on Sunday morning. Any Christian concerned with evangelism must be concerned with the application of the Gospel to the social and economic order. For the acid test of the power of Christ to transform individual life is what it does to the man or the woman in personal, social and economic relations. There is where non-Christian people look most often and most carefully.

Presbyterians believe, as the Bible teaches, that men are known by their fruits. They believe in putting faith to work right where people live. They do not retreat into dogmas declared by the church or an orthodoxy which limits itself to one particular type of evangelism. They believe in witnessing to their faith by every means in every area of life. Some Presbyterians need to be reminded of the importance of their testimony on the frontiers where they would be most effective.

2. Through the Application of Christian Principles

What has been said leads to a further emphasis on the fact that a part of the evangelistic and educational work of the Christian witness is the application of Christian principles to all of the relationships of life. Even though we might not follow John Calvin, the founder of modern Presbyterianism, in seeking directly to control civic life, we do recognize the fact that he sought to bring the teachings of the Bible to bear on the total life of the people in Geneva. He did it by authority granted by the Council and the people of Geneva. We do it by persuasion. When we fail to do it by persuasion, we and our children suffer the consequences.

The difficulties of winning persons to Christ in a non-Christian society are well known to Christian missionaries in lands where Christians are very much in the minority. Russian controlled China in a few years will probably be a very hard field for missionaries to re-enter. The society in which we live is gradually imposing its lax ideas and practices on church people. There is a constant struggle between the church and the world for the control of the ideas and habits of a people. *Unless the church is constantly transforming the world, it will gradually conform to the world.*

Let us suppose, for example, that a Christian employer resents the intervention of organized forces not among his employees to a point where he refuses to play fair with his employees. Because other people are un-Christian and are acting from selfish motives, must he become like them? Or must he play fair even though he does not like some of the means used by outside forces?

Again, imagine that a workman is required to join a union in order to secure work. He finds that instead of going on the principle that an honest day's work should be given for a full day's pay, he goes on the principle that he is to do as little as possible for as much return as he can get. Will not such practice eventually shoot prices up to where he and his family suffer and inflation destroys the earning power he might have had?

Quite obviously it is very hard to be Christian in the workaday world in which people live. Why? Is it not because Presbyterians and others have waited to be pushed in many directions because they did not take the lead in establishing Christian principles in business? There are some men who have done just that and have been successful in spite of all of the pressures brought to bear upon them. They are the stabilizing influences on economy and business. They put Christian principles to work insofar as they can in an un-Christian society.

Suppose again, business men are asked to contribute to the Community Chest. They start out with a cocktail party and celebrate with a similar party at the end. Certain Christian men suggest that they will support this movement only if they can seek God's blessing upon it and the way it is conducted. Their testimony becomes effective in changing habits. This is the application of Christian principles to society. Society is in some measure transformed through Christian individuals who take their responsibility as Christians seriously.

The logic of refusing to take Christian principles into busines and government and international relations is the logic of letting a world become more and more pagan while the Church is trying to develop in it a minority of persons who should become more and more Christian. It is the logic of serving a man whiskey to get his business and then working in Alcoholics Anonymous to cure him of his habit of drink. If Presbyterians expect to give an effective witness to Christ in their world, they must put Christian principles to work in that world. For the power of the Gospel can work there as it works in the individual.

3. Through the Abiding Worship and Service of the Church

It is easy to forget the unostentatious but continuous influence of the regular worship and service of the church. People in the United States who take the church for granted do not recognize the importance of this influence. Why is it that a person may leave his house unguarded for hours at a time while he goes to his work? It is because of the influence of the church on society. Why may a woman drive in safety from morning until night on the highways of our state and nation? Because of the influence of the church on society. Why is a contract considered binding upon two parties? Because of the influence of the church on the laws of our land and on the ideals of business life. Why may one borrow money or buy with credit to furnish his house? Because at least most of the people in our society have directly or indirectly inherited the values of the life and work of the church.

It is no accident that our founding fathers built a church before they built their homes. They knew that without their regular worship and work, they would soon be fighting among themselves. Their survival depended upon their willingness to forget their own selfish interest in the common good. Presbyterians believe in regular worship and service. They believe in it to an extent that they invest millions of dollars each year on local and benevolent expenses. They send out elders to conduct services in chapels and outposts if there are not enough ordained ministers to do the job. They work with migrants, with coal miners, with mountaineers, with the most cultured and the least cultured members of society. They know that the regular worship and service of the church changes society through changing individuals who exert their influence on society.

[112]

Our task in modern society is tremendously great because we have been neglecting many opportunities to witness effectively to our faith in Christ. It is also great because our world has become one world and the relationships of life have become proportionately complex. We have a challenging task which may be done within the framework of our time-honored principle of separation between church and state. Let us witness and persuade in the name and in the power of Jesus Christ. He will be with us always, even as He promised to those who took His commands seriously.

WORKSHEET

1. In our previous study of the visible church, we recognized the fact that the church is a part of human society. Ordinarily men are saved through the ministry of the_____, and need the church for their best_____and_____.

2. While persons are saved as_____through their faith in Christ, they have an obligation to_____to their faith in the society of which they are a part.

3. While it is true that John Calvin used governmental powers to reform the society of Geneva, American Christians follow the principle of _____to secure voluntary cooperation rather than the principle of_____to enforce Christian ideals on society.

4. Because some people have exercised a social concern without being actively identified with the Christian church, some Christians have tended to draw back from their_____in bringing the Gospel of Christ to bear upon the problems and the life of society.

5 Some Presbyterians have assumed that there is a distinction to be made between the _____Gospel and the_____ Gospel.

6. The redemptive work of Christ in society comes about first of all through the_____ and _____ of individuals in society.

7. The redemptive work of Christ in society is also made more effective through the_____of Christian principles to the relationships of everyday life in society.

8. If the church refuses to put Christian principles to work in the social order, it will find the world becoming more and more pagan while the church is striving to make its members more and more Christian.

9. The abiding_____and_____of the church is an important means of bringing the power of the Gospel to bear on the social order.

[113]

CHAPTER XII

Our Expectation of Future Life

INTRODUCTION

The affirmation of the Apostles' Creed, "I believe in the life everlast-ing," has not been very clearly understood by Christian people as a whole. They live on the earth. Their thinking tends to be of the earth. So they say when the body of some loved one is laid in a grave, "He is dead." Or, "She died, and I have no hope left."

Such statements belie the truth of the Bible. The concept of person-ality in the Bible teaches us to say, "I am a soul (personality, being), and I have a body." Some people say just the reverse: "I am a body, and I have a soul." If the latter statement be true, it means that the real person is a human body and that the soul is something that person has in his possession. This is not true from the point of view of the Bible. I am a living soul, made so by the creator, and reborn to eternal life through my faith in Christ. He has given me a physical body through physical birth. I have this body, but I am not limited to this body except in my life on earth.

Again, in the Gospel of John we have two words used for *life*. One is the word *psuche*, which means life in the physical body. A dog or a cat may have this kind of life. It is the life which comes through the normal functioning of the organs of the body. Examples of the use of this word may be found in John 15:13 and 10:17. Men in battle give up their lives for their country. The other word for *life* is the word *zoe*, which is the life of God made available to believers in Jesus Christ as Lord and Saviour. Examples of the use of this word may be found in John 1:4; 10:10 and 3:16. Of the seventeen times this word is used in John's Gospel, twelve times the word *eternal* or *everlasting* is used to describe it. Not once is this adjective applied to the word psuche. This is significant, for it reveals that while the life of the physical body is not regarded as eternal, the spiritual life of God in believers is eternal.

A. THE RELATION OF THE LIFE HERE TO THE LIFE HEREAFTER

In the light of what has been said, eternal life is a quality of life which belongs to believers here as well as hereafter. It is the life of God given to believers through Jesus Christ. It comes to believers through reproduction of Christ's life in them, not through their efforts to imitate Him. As is so clearly stated in John 3:1-21, the birth from above is the necessary means by which this new life is experienced. It is like taking a cutting from a rosebush and rooting it in rich soil where

[114]

it will grow and bloom like the parent rose. It is like the union of the Spirit of God with Mary to produce the Son of God in the flesh. So also the Spirit of God unites with the heart of the believer to reproduce His life in the experience of men.

Eternal life does not begin after physical death. It begins when the life of God is given to believers. As stated in John 5:24, the one who believes shall not come into judgment, but has already passed from death into life.

This means that life on earth is the testing ground which determines who will become believers and who will not. Life after death is a continuation of life here. But it is a continuation in a richer and larger way, without the weaknesses of the flesh to deter us. The point of view which has been expressed is well summarized in the Shorter Catechism, Answers to Questions 37 and 38:

"The souls of believers are at their death made perfect in holiness, and, do immediately pass into glory; and their bodies, being still united to Christ, do rest in their graves till the resurrection."

"At the resurrection, believers, being raised up in glory, shall be openly acknowledged, and acquitted in the day of judgment, and made perfectly blessed in the full enjoyment of God to all eternity."

B. THE BODY OF BELIEVERS HERE AND HEREAFTER

We are sure of the fact that we have physical bodies suited to life here. We are not so sure of the kind of bodies we shall have hereafter. The message of Paul in I Corinthians 15:20-58 is instructive at this point. In reply to the direct question, With what body do they come? (verse 35), Paul answers that God gives a resurrection body according to His own wishes and pleasure. This body will be appropriate to the kind of life involved. Just as the grain of wheat dies to become a stalk which reproduces the grain, so the perishable earthly body is replaced with an imperishable body. The physical body is replaced with a spiritual body. Even for those who shall be alive in the flesh at the end, there will be a change of body from the earthly to the heavenly, from the physical to the spiritual.

We get some cues about the kind of bodies we shall have from the resurrection body of the risen Lord. He was not limited by time or space, but appeared and disappeared. From the experience of the risen Lord we gain confidence in the resurrection of our own bodies. In the words of the Apostle's Creed we say, "I believe in the resurrection of the body." Our Confession points to a final day when the bodies of the earth shall be somehow reunited with the souls of believers in the words:

"At the last day, such as are found alive shall not die, but be changed: and all the dead shall be raised up with the self-same bodies, and none other, although with different qualities, which shall be united again to their souls for ever." (Chapter XXXIV, Article II.)

This doctrine, it should be stated in all frankness, is not easy to understand. But we may be sure that the creator is able to do for us all things well. He who transforms our personalities can easily transform the bodies that we leave behind in a grave. But the glorious truth is that while our bodies are changed, we live eternally with Christ in glory. That our bodies shall be like His is suggested in Chapter XXXIV; Article III of the Confession of Faith:

"The bodies of the unjust shall, by the power of Christ, be raised to dishonor; the bodies of the just, by His Spirit, unto honor, and be made conformable to His glorious body."

C. THE RETURN OF CHRIST

Relatively little is said in scripture about the return of Christ, and still less in the Presbyterian Standards. In Chapter VIII, Article IV, this line appears: "and shall return to judge men and angels, at the end of the world." (Compare answer to Question 28 of Shorter Catechism.) However, a fuller statement is given in the answer to Question 56 of the Larger Catechism:

"Christ is to be exalted in his coming again to judge the world, in that He, who was unjustly judged and condemned by wicked men, shall come again at the last day in great power, and in the full manifestation of his own glory, and of his Father's, with all his holy angels, with a shout, with the voice of the archangel, and with the trumpet of God, to judge the world in righteousness."

It is clear from the above statement that Presbyterians believe in the return of Christ. The promises made by our Lord that He would return have been received at face value. The statement of Jesus concerning the time of His coming is also received as authoritative. "But of that day and hour no one knows, not even the angels of heaven, nor the Son, but the Father only." (Matthew 24:36.) Since these words were spoken by the Son in the flesh, it is both possible and likely that He shares this knowledge with the Father now.

The passages in the Gospels that obviously deal with the return of Christ (Matthew 24:36-51; Mark 13:24-27, 32-37; Luke 12:35-48; John 14:1-3) teach Jesus' followers to live expectantly and faithfully. While no one knows when He will return, all are to be faithfully doing their tasks as though He will return at any moment. No one is to assume that because His coming is delayed, it will always be delayed.

[116]

Whether He returns in our lifetime, or in millions of years, we are nearer that great day than we were yesterday. It may be today or tomorrow or in the distant future. But it is certain and should be prepared for at any moment.

1. THE STANDARDS NOT EXPLICIT CONCERNING DETAILS OF CHRIST'S RETURN

Some Presbyterians may ask why the Confession is not more explicit than it is concerning the time and the manner of Christ's return. It is because the scriptures are not explicit about the time and because they teach that He will return on the clouds with great power and glory (note the poetic way of expressing this truth). To be sure, many interpreters of the Bible have tried to fill in the details, even to setting the time. But each one so far has been wrong. The average for correctness is zero even though the confident affirmations of certainty have been very high. Therefore, both because the Confession is careful in its statement and because the scriptures themselves are indefinite as to time (unless one assumes that they were written for our day and not for the nineteen centuries intervening, which is quite an assumption concerning our importance in God's sight), many Presbyterian ministers are guarded in setting any specific time for Christ's return. They are not ignorant concerning the events of the present day, but they are aware of the fact that in other centuries from the first to the twentieth, events have been many times very similar for Europeans and Americans (if these were God's primary concern) to present events.

Of course, this does not satisfy the curious speculators who want everything concerning the future worked out in a neat little package of theology. But the very brevity of the statement in the Larger Catechism leaves room for variety in expectation. It sometimes permits matters of opinion to become matters of faith. History has proved the danger of such practice. The Millerites of 1843 and 1844, who set a specific time for Christ's return, and who found that they were wrong, not only lost face, but most of them lost their faith. This is the danger to be avoided. Let those who will, become definite as to the year or the lifetime in which Christ will return. Let all Presbyterians and all Christians live expectantly and faithfully, knowing that Christ will return either today or tomorrow or at such future time as God the Father sees fit.

It should be recognized further that the Larger Catechism does not elaborate on a system of events associated with the return of Christ. Nor do the scriptures until they are made to fit into a scheme already worked out and imposed upon them. One gets the impression from reading the Revelation, chapter 20, that the inspired writer follows his usual custom in the book by painting pictures with words. Verses 1-3 deal with the binding of Satan for a thousand years, and verses 7-11 tell of the final destruction of Satan after the thousand years are finished. Verses 4-6 seem to be describing the victory of the saints during the thousand years referred to in verses 1-3. Verses 11-15 describe the final judgment which logically and apparently chronologically follows the preceding verses. This chapter, as the writer has ·indicated elsewhere,* should be interpreted as a part of the book as a whole. It gives no clear indication of many of the charted or imaginary events that some men have associated with the second coming of Christ. It points to the return of Christ before the final judgment. Whether this return is literally one thousand years before the final judgment, or whether it follows exactly a thousand years of the coming of Christ in the hearts of men is a matter of interpretation.

2. THE MILLENARIAN VIEWS OF CHRIST'S RETURN

For those who would ask, "What is the difference between premillenialism, postmillenialism, and amillenialism?", we would make the following reply. Premillenialism is a point of view which holds that Christ will return to the earth before (pre) the thousand year reign of Christ begins. Postmillenialism is a point of view which holds that Christ will return to the earth after (post) a thousand year reign of Christ in the hearts of men. Amillenialism is a point of view which refuses to literalize the thousand year period as being significant in one's doctrine concerning the return of Christ. A person may be one of the three and still be a good Presbyterian.

In a previous chapter on the church we have dealt with the other question that ordinarily arises. It concerns the refusal of the Presbyterian church to accept dispensationalism. Some congregations are dispensational in their point of view. On the whole, dispensationalists are in the minority in most of the churches where they are active. The 1944 Assembly adopted a report which set forth the reasons why dispensationalism is not approved in the Presbyterian church. This report is available at your nearest Presbyterian bookstore.

Our concern here is to present the Presbyterian belief in the return of Christ. We repeat the fact that the Presbyterian Standards do not propose any specific system of interpretation concerning the return of Christ. They do teach that He will return to judge the whole world in God's good time. They also teach that men are to remain faithful and watchful as they await His coming. In the words of the Confession of Faith, Chapter XXXV, Article III:

"As Christ would have us to be certainly persuaded that there shall be a day of judgment, both to deter all men from sin, and for the

---

*How to Study the Revelation, pages 92-99.

greater consolation of the godly in their adversity: so will he have that day unknown to men, that they may shake off all carnal security, and be always watchful, because they know not at what hour the Lord will come; and may be ever prepared to say, Come, Lord Jesus, come quickly. Amen."

D. THE LAST JUDGMENT

Four things may be said about the last judgment. First, it is the judgment of Christ. Second, it is universal. Third, it is according to the thoughts, words and deeds done in the flesh. Fourth, it is final. Chapter XXXV of the Confession of Faith deals with this final judgment. It presents the basic doctrines we propose to discuss.

1. It Is the Judgment of Christ

In the Gospel, Jesus Christ is presented as Lord and Saviour. This is the teaching of the scriptures. This is the belief of the Christian church. He remains the Saviour as long as men live in the flesh. But in the final judgment Christ is the judge. He is fair and reasonable, but He is the judge. He will not forget that men are saved by faith, but will remember that their faith always expresses itself, not merely in words, but also in deeds. He will judge all men by the fruit of their faith as it is expressed in their deeds.

2. It Is Universal

The final judgment includes apostate angels and all persons who have lived upon the earth. It includes both the wicked and the righteous, both the dead and those who are then living. No one shall escape this righteous judgment. All humanity will be gathered before the throne of God. The saints whose robes are washed in the blood of the Lamb will stand before Him whom they have loved and served. The sinners who have refused to accept His pardon will likewise stand before Him whose love they have repudiated. The hypocrites will be there, who gave a show of religion, but whose hearts were far from God. The sincere but unsung heroes and heroines of the faith will be there, surprised perhaps at their feeling of "at-homeness." but gazing with wonder and appreciation at the face of Him whom they have served. You and I will be there too, standing with our common humanity before the judgment bar of God.

3. It Is According to the Thoughts, Words, and Deeds of Men

Sometimes people tend to separate themselves into several compartments, as though the way they think may be the opposite of what they say or do. From experience many persons know that such a thing is possible. But it is possible as a habit only at the expense of warping personality. Before God there can be no such division, for He knows the secret intents and thoughts of the heart.

Jesus' most dramatic description of the final judgment is recorded in the parable of the judgment in Matthew 25:31-46. He pictures all the nations standing before the judgment throne. To those who have served Him by serving others, He gives the invitation to inherit the eternal Kingdom prepared for them. To those whose faith does not get expressed in an appropriate service for others, He will give sentence to depart to the eternal fire prepared for the devil and his angels. For Jesus knew that one's deepest and most determining thoughts will find expression in the way one lives. Faith is the rootage of conduct, but conduct is the fruitage of faith. We are saved *by* faith *for* good works in His name. We are judged according to the way we express the deep faith that is in our hearts.

4. It Is Final

Nowhere in the scriptures is there the promise of a chance to determine one's eternal destiny after he departs this life. In fact, Luke 16:19-31 tells a story which indicates clearly that there is no chance of a change in decision about one's destiny after this life. A great chasm or gulf is fixed between those who receive the reward of their faith and those who receive the consequences of their careless unbelief. No one can cross over either way. The doctrine of purgatory did not originate in scripture. It originated in an entirely different source. This is why Presbyterians refuse to accept it. The judgment of men on earth is final.

In like fashion the final judgment settles things once for all. The parable in Matthew 25:31-46 makes no mention of anything other than a final judgment. A similar picture is drawn in the Revelation 20:11-15. Human personality of one kind in this life need not be expected to change magically into something else. We become more and more like ourselves as each day passes. So finally we come to the last judgment when our reward will be confirmed for eternity and our wickedness will be judged in eternity. Let us pray earnestly for ourselves and those we love that we may be united in joyous worship and service about His throne.

E. THE EXPERIENCE OF THE RIGHTEOUS AND THE WICKED IN ETERNITY

The Confession describes this experience in the following words: "For then shall the righteous go into everlasting life, and receive that fulness of joy and refreshing which shall come from the presence of the Lord: but the wicked, who know not God, and obey not the Gospel of Jesus Christ, shall be cast into eternal torments, and punished with everlasting destruction from the presence of the Lord, and from the glory of His power." (Chapter XXXV, Article II.)

Chapters 21 and 22 of the Revelation give a poetic and vivid description of the new Jerusalem, which is our nearest approach to a picture of heaven. Everything is new in the new city of God. The water of life is freely offered to all who wish to receive it. Sonship to God for those who live victoriously is the blessed inheritance of the redeemed. Worship and service in the city of eternal light will consume the time of those who love Christ. All that is glorious and wonderful will belong to those who have loved and served their Lord.

"But as for the cowardly, the faithless, the polluted, as for murderers, fornicators, sorcerers, idolaters, and all liars, their lot shall be in the lake that burns with fire and brimstone, which is the second death." (Revelation 21:8.)

Whether we think of hell in terms of distance or of difference from the experience of heaven, we know that the remorse and the torment of unbelievers is terrible. We do not consider an eternal heaven merely because it is pleasant or an eternal hell simply because it is unpleasant. We accept both because they are taught in the word of God. Again we suggest fervent prayer that all of God's own may respond in faith to the glorious Gospel of salvation in Jesus Christ.

In this chapter we have discussed a number of things about which we have only a limited knowledge. We do have enough knowledge for our salvation and our growth in grace. We also know that our Lord is able to keep all that we have committed unto Him, and that He will do all things for His glory and for our good. In this confidence let us find peace and rest for our souls, and let us live expectantly as we await the end of our days or the coming of our Lord.

WORKSHEET

1. The Christian person makes the following assertions:

    a. I am a living_____and I have a physical_____.

    b. The life in the body is temporal, but the life of the believer is

    _____.

2. The life in the present is the_____for the life to come.

3. The body of believers hereafter will be suited to the kind of_____ that believers will experience hereafter.

4. Presbyterians believe in the return of Christ whether or not they set

    the _____of His return.

5. Because we know so little about the future life, we are sometimes tempted to speculate about it. We must be careful to keep the

   _____as our guide of faith and life.

6. The three views about the return of Christ which are held by many Presbyterians may be defined as follows:

   a. Premillenialism _____

   _____.

   b. Postmillenialism _____

   _____.

   c. Amillenialism _____

   _____.

7. Presbyterians are urged to be_____in performing their duties even though they do not know when Christ will return.

8. Presbyterians believe the following things about the last judgment:

   a.

   b.

   c.

   d.

9. Presbyterians believe that the righteous will be_____ and that the wicked will be_____in eternity.

CHAPTER XIII

Our Affirmation of Faith

INTRODUCTION

Persons who have studied the topics discussed thus far should have a clearer understanding of what Presbyterians believe. This series of studies has not treated every part of the Presbyterian Standards, but has lifted out for scrutiny at least most of the major doctrines taught in these standards. The interpretation which has been given may not satisfy each person at every point, but it should have encouraged readers to re-examine the Standards for themselves. The important questions that must be answered now are these: where do we go from here? What use shall we make of the information received and the doctrines understood?

This closing chapter will appeal for a demonstration of faith by action. As James says: "Show me your faith apart from your works, and I by my works will show you my faith." (James 2:18b.) Let us examine a few of the ways that we may show our faith in these things by our daily living. Here are some ways we may declare our faith:

A. IN THE SCRIPTURES BY DILIGENT STUDY

Presbyterians claim with other Protestant bodies that the Bible is their rule of faith and life. But how shall they know what this rule is unless they learn to use it?

Suppose for a moment that a carpenter wished to build a house. Suppose that he had a carpenter's rule and square. But suppose he cut his timbers and tried to put them together without measuring and marking them properly with his rule and square. What kind of house would he build? How many of you would want to buy such a house? Obviously very few. The same is true of those who would be building Christian lives. It is not enough to possess a Bible as the rule of faith and life. Christians must use it properly. They must study diligently by the best methods to demonstrate that they are approved by God. Only so will they be able to hold a straight course in God's word of truth. (See II Timothy 2:15.)

One of the features of the work we strive to do together is to develop earnest and intelligent students of the Bible. This is not an end in itself, but a means toward letting the Bible and its redemptive message come to life in the experience of believers. We propose to restore the Bible to the laity of the church by helping them to learn better how to use it. Let all who believe in the Bible as the rule of faith and life demonstrate that faith by reverent, regular, diligent study. And let that study issue in the building of a mature life through the guidance and power of the Spirit of God.

B. IN GOD BY FAITH AND OBEDIENCE

A recent survey reports that ninety-nine per cent of the people in America believe in some kind of supreme being. But this does not mean that they really believe in the Hebrew-Christian God, for at least half of them have little or no part in the worship and work of synagogue and church. They may believe that such a God exists, but do not believe always that they are bound to such a God by faith and obedience.

As has been indicated earlier in these studies, the God in whom Presbyterians believe does demand faith and obedience. It is of little moment to declare, "I believe in a sovereign God" unless we are also willing to affirm, "He is and shall be Lord of my life." This is the crucial test of faith. Jesus Himself said, "Not every one who says to me, 'Lord, Lord,' shall enter the kingdom of heaven, but he who does the will of my Father who is in heaven." (Matthew 7:21.)

To declare our faith in God is therefore to commit ourselves to discover, to do and to keep on doing the will of the Father day by day. What is God's will in my social life? What is God's will in my home life? What is God's will in my church life? What is God's will in my business life? These are the questions that must be answered reverently and purposefully if we are to declare our faith in God. To say we believe in God and then to live as though He were neither sovereign nor important is to make the same hollow mockery of faith that the Pharisees did in Jesus' day. Our Lord's severest woes were pronounced upon them. What would He say to us? Let us declare our faith in God by our obedience to His revealed will in Jesus Christ our Lord.

C. IN CHRIST BY CLAIMING SALVATION

The twentieth century has been marked by many efforts to define the nature of Jesus Christ. Some have written with all the skill they could muster to prove that He was only a great and saintly man. They insist that the difference between Jesus and others is that He was more sensitive to God than others are. Some Jewish scholars have attempted to prove that Jesus was a Jewish prophet, but no more. Others have sought to do Him credit by insisting upon His deity even at the expense of His humanity. Even Presbyterians have sometimes been carried out of their way with these winds of doctrine. To a greater or lesser degree we have done everything with Christ in the twentieth century except commit ourselves to Him.

Presbyterians believe that God offers salvation in Christ, but they find it harder to take salvation so that it will become God's gift. It is only an offer until it is taken and used for the purpose for which the Gospel was intended. Here is a man, for instance, who would like to be saved, but he simply cannot bring his intellectual pride to the point of taking salvation by faith. Or here is another who is not living faithfully with his wife. He would like to do it, but old habits have him involved in relationships that he cannot leave alone. Salvation means taking all such relationships to Christ in genuine repentance and taking Christ into all the relationships that one continues.

Here again is a woman who has fought for her measure of security by driving her husband in business. Then he becomes ill and she has to face the possibility of reducing the family income to half its former amount. She may easily lose her faith in God because of the terrible thing that she thinks has happened to her. In such a case pride over losing the social position gained through economic success may keep her from committing herself and her husband anew to God in Christ. And she may miss the salvation of her soul because of the things that have claimed so much of her life.

What our world needs more than anything else is a demonstration of the power of Jesus Christ to work out salvation in a human life. This demonstration of power comes through taking His grace and using it with the problems we face. To declare our faith is to take the salvation He offers, to work out our salvation with constant fear and much trembling, being fully conscious all the while that God is working within us to will and accomplish His good pleasure. (See Philippians 2:12, 13.) God works through our cooperative effort to make us witnesses of His power. Let Presbyterians declare their faith in Christ by taking and using the power of God unto salvation.

D. IN THE CHURCH BY REALIZING ITS MISSION

Too many Presbyterians have come to look upon their church as a field rather than a force. It is a field for winning converts to Christ and for making Christians more mature in Christ. But the purpose of such endeavor is to train and provide a working force for Christ. For it is well demonstrated in history that unless the church is constantly overcoming the world, the world will constantly be degenerating the church. The church has no alternative but to carry the Gospel of Jesus Christ into all the world. These are its marching orders. It cannot abide in the tents of inactivity and expect the battle of the Lord to be won.

Nor can the church achieve its mission by enlisting in its regular worship and service less than half of its members. Who really believes in the church and seldom if ever engages in its regular activities? How seriously do we take the mission of the church when it takes at least twenty-five church members to win one convert a year? Have we not drifted into an idea that the church is an organization for our convenience and enjoyment rather than a fellowship with a worldwide mission?

A wild duck once flew down into a barnyard and wintered there on the good food which was provided. In the spring he heard the call of his mates overhead on their migration northward, and rose to meet them in the air. But his wings were flabby and his weight was burdensome. Soon he came back to the barnyard, flying about in it to prove that he could have flown with his mates if he wanted to. But the next time they passed overhead he remembered his former failure and refused to try it. In due time he was on a platter in the kitchen.

This is a parable of the church. It was made to proclaim the Christian Gospel just as the wild duck was made to fly. When it becomes self-satisfied, it loses its power to march and in due time it is overcome by other forces in the world. Let all who believe in the church declare that faith by helping it to perform its important mission.

E. IN THE HOME BY MAKING IT MORE CHRISTIAN

During the last two decades the church has rediscovered the home. But it has not yet completed the task of enlisting the home in the redemptive work of God in the world. Many years of taking responsibility from the home and of showing limited concern for the home have created a spiritual vacuum in many homes and have left a gap between the church and the home. Yet because of the time spent there and because of the effectiveness of parental example, the home holds an overwhelming edge on the church as a means of Christian nurture. Since the church is made up of members from the homes of the congregation, it is as strong as the homes which make it up.

It is quite obvious that to make homes more Christian is to make churches more effective. Changing the home must begin at home. This change comes about when parents agree to do something about it and follow up their purpose with constructive action. We can affirm our faith by living it day by day. Fascist and nazi and communist movements make the state the center of a child's interest and activity. Christianity centers its emphasis on the home as an ally of the church. If we surrender the home by default, we will invite some pagan way of life to take it over. If we make it a powerful force for Christ, we will declare our faith that the Christian home, like the home from which our Lord came, is God's appointed center of Christian nurture and growth.

F. IN SOCIETY BY PRACTICING OUR GOSPEL

The plea of our world is for a religion that will work. And it is for a religion that will work where working people live. Communism is made to work in areas where it is feared. It is ruthless and efficient.

We believe that we have something much better than communism. But we must make it work voluntarily or it will not work at all. The Roman Catholic church, following a pattern of organization similar to that used in totalitarian states, brings pressure from the top to make certain of its principles work. Presbyterianism is democratic in that it seeks to have the will of the church express itself voluntarily through the activities of its members. But unless Presbyterianism has a religion that can be made to work, it becomes discounted among those who might be won for Christ.

The Presbyterian church does not have a neat social program for the world. It does have a social conscience. This conscience must find expression in business, in politics, in race relations, in labor and management relations, and in every other relation in which Presbyterians live. It must be a keen and sensitive conscience. It must be a Christian conscience. It must be an educated conscience. It must be a conscience which dares to lay hold on the redemptive power of God in Jesus Christ. It must never limit the power of this Gospel to a few small areas of life, but must take Christ into every area and relationship in life. Only so will religion be made to work. Only so will we declare our faith in the power of Christ to transform our society through transformed individuals in society.

G. IN THE FUTURE BY LIVING ETERNALLY IN TIME

Some Christians face eternity as though it were less important than time. The things of the earth seem to them so important that the things of heaven are matters only of whim or convenience. They have missed the very essence of eternal life. For eternal life is not something which begins after death, but something which begins when a believer is born anew in the Kingdom of God. From that time forward he has the life of God within him. This life must be permitted to grow to maturity through the means God has appointed. But it is eternal.

This means that everything the Christian does each day should have some significance for eternity. The smile to the conductor on the street car, the reply to the letter that rubs the wrong way, the zest with which the business conference is approached, the faithfulness with which the daily service is rendered, all have an eternal significance. They are like pebbles dropped in a lake which forms a series of everwidening ripples moving outward. The writing of these lines has an eternal significance because it is done in the name of Christ for the glory of God and the service of believers.

Nearly two thousand years ago the Son of God prayed in a garden and died on a cross. The third day He rose again from the dead. These events occurred on specific days in specific years. But they started a series of redemptive waves that have reached to the shores of our own lives and hearts. They had a significance for eternity. So also do our acts of service in His name. Because His life is within, everything you do is eternal. Make it worthy of Christ throughout eternity.

WORKSHEET

1. James 2:18b suggests:_____
_____.

2. We may affirm our faith in the scriptures by_____ _____.

3. We may affirm our faith in God by_____and_____.

4. We may affirm our faith in Christ by_____ _____ _____.

5. We may affirm our faith in the church by_____its_____.

6. We may affirm our faith in the home by_____it more
_____.

7. We may affirm our faith in society by_____our_____.

8. We may affirm our faith in the future by_____eternally in time.

9. Write a paragraph or two telling the best things you have learned in this series of studies.